T0323133

THE BARBARY CORSAIRS.

First published in 1890 by T. Fisher Unwin

This reprint published by
Darf Publishers Limited

First edition 1890
New impression 1984

ALGIERS, 1700.

(*From a Map in the British Museum.*)

THE BARBARY
CORSAIRS

BY

STANLEY LANE-POOLE

AUTHOR OF "THE LIFE OF LORD STRATFORD DE REDCLIFFE," "TURKEY,"
"THE MOORS IN SPAIN," ETC., ETC.

WITH ADDITIONS BY LIEUT. J. D. J. KELLEY, U.S. NAVY

London

DARF PUBLISHERS LIMITED
1984

Printed and bound in Great Britain by
A. Wheaton & Co., Ltd, Exeter

ISBN 1 85077 018 2

CONTENTS.

CONTENTS.

XII.

XIII.

XIV.

PART II.

THE PETTY PIRATES.

XV.

XVI.

XVII.

CONTENTS.

LIST OF ILLUSTRATIONS.

. These illustrations are chiefly reproduced from *La Sphère des deux Mondes*, composée en François, par Darinel pasteur des Amadis, Anvers, 1555; Furttenbach's *Architectura Navalis*, 1629; Dan's *Histoire de Barbarie*, 1637; Ogilby's *Africa*, 1670; Adm. Jurien de la Gravière's *Derniers Jours de la Marine à Rames*; and the maps [63842. (3.)—S. 9. 9. (39).—S. 10. 2.—64162. (2.)—64043. (1.)] in the British Museum.

LIST OF THE PRINCIPAL AUTHORITIES CONSULTED.

BATŪTA, IBN-: *Voyages.* Ed. Defrémery. 4 vols. Paris. 1874 9.

BRAITHWAITE, J.: *History of the Revolutions in the Empire of Morocco upon the death of the late Emperor Muley Ishmael.* 1729.

BRANTÔME, P. DE BOURDEILLE, SEIGN. DE.: *Hommes illustres. Œuvres,* Vols. 1 and 2. Paris. 1822.

BROADLEY, A. M.: *Tunis, Past and Present.* 2 vols. 1882.

CELESIA, E.: *Conspiracy of Fieschi.* E. T. 1866.

CERVANTES: *Don Quixote.* Trans. H. E. Watts. 5 vols. 1888-9.

CHENIER, L. S.: *Present State of the Empire of Morocco.* E. T. 1788
Cruelties of the Algerine Pirates. 1816.

DAN, PÈRE F.: *Histoire de Barbarie et de ses Corsaires.* 2nd ed. Paris. 1649.

EDRĪSĪ, EL-: *Description de l'Afrique et de l'Espagne.* Edd. Dozy and De Goeje. Leyden. 1866.

FROISSART, J.: *Chronicles.* Trans. T. Johnes. 2 vols. 1844.

FURTTENBACH, J.: *Architectura Navalis: das ist, Von dem Schiff-Gebaw, auf dem Meer und Seekusten zu Gebrauchen.* Ulm. 1629.

GRAVIÈRE, Adm. JURIEN DE LA: *Les Derniers Jours de la Marine à Rames.* Paris. 1885.
,, : *Doria et Barberousse.* 1886.
,, : *Les Corsaires Barbaresques.* 1887.
,, : *Les Chevaliers de Malte,* 2 vols. 1887.
,, : *La Guerre de Chypre,* 2 vols. 1888.

GRAMMONT, H.: *Histoire d'Alger.* 1887.

HAEDO, DIEGO DE: *Topographia e Historia General de Argel.* Valladolid. 1612.

HĀJJI KHALĪFA: *History of the Maritime Wars of the Turks.*

HAMMER, J. VON.: *Geschichte des Osmanischen Reiches.* 2nd ed. 4 vols. Festh. 1834-6.

1 *

Journal Asiatique: Ser. II., iv., xii.; III., xi., xii., xiii.; IV., iii., v., vii., x., xviii.; V., ii., v., vi., xii., xiii.; VI., xviii.; VII., vii.

MARMOL, LUYS DEL CARAVAJAL: *Descripcion de Africa.* Granada. 1573.

MAS-LATRIE, COMTE DE: *Relations et commerce de l'Afrique Septentrionale (ou Magreb) avec les nations chrétiennes au moyen âge.* Paris. 1886.

MORGAN, J.: *A complete History of Algiers.* 1731.

PLAYFAIR, Sir R. L.: *The Scourge of Christendom.* 1884.

RECLUS, ELISÉE: *Nouvelle Géographie Universelle.* XI. Paris. *Registre des Prises.* Algiers. 1872.

ROUSSEAU, Baron A.: *Annales Tunisiennes.* Algiers. 1864.

    ,,   : *History of the Conquest of Tunis by the Ottomans.* 1883.

SHAW, T.: *Travels in Barbary and the Levant.* 3rd ed. Edinb. 1808.

WINDUS, J.: *Journey to Mequinez.* 1725.

INTRODUCTION.

THE BARBARY CORSAIRS.

I.

THE REVENGE OF THE MOORS.

FOR more than three centuries the trading nations
of Europe were suffered to pursue their commerce
or forced to abandon their gains at the bidding of
pirates. From the days when Barbarossa defied the
whole strength of the Emperor Charles V., to the
early part of the present century, when prizes were
taken by Algerine rovers under the guns, so to say,
of all the fleets of Europe, the Corsairs were masters
of the narrow seas, and dictated their own terms to
all comers. Nothing but the creation of the large
standing navies of the present age crippled them ;
nothing less than the conquest of their too convenient coasts could have thoroughly suppressed
them. During those three centuries they levied
blackmail upon all who had any trading interest in
the Mediterranean. The Venetians, Genoese, Pisans
in older days ; the English, French, Dutch, Danish,
Swedish, and American Governments in modern
times, purchased security by the payment of a re-

gular tribute, or by the periodical presentation of costly gifts. The penalty of resistance was too well known to need exemplification ; thousands of Christian slaves in the bagnios at Algiers bore witness to the consequences of an independent policy. So long as the nations of Europe continued to quarrel among themselves, instead of presenting a united line of battle to the enemy, such humiliations had to be endured ; so long as a Corsair raid upon Spain suited the policy of France ; so long as the Dutch, in their jealousy of other states, could declare that Algiers was necessary to them ; there was no chance of the plague subsiding ; and it was not till the close of the great Napoleonic wars that the Powers agreed, at the Congress of Aix la Chapelle in 1818, to act together, and do away with the scourge of Christendom. And even then little was accomplished till France combined territorial aggrandizement with the *rôle* of a civilizing influence.

There had been pirates in the Mediterranean long before the Turks took up the trade ; indeed, ever since boats were built their capabilities for plunder must have been realized. The filibustering expedition of Jason and the loot of the Golden Fleece is an early instance, and the Greeks at all times have distinguished themselves by acting up to Jason's example by sea and land. The Moslems, however, were some time in accustoming themselves to the perils of the deep. At first they marvelled greatly at " those that go down to the sea in ships, and have their business in great waters," but they did not hasten to follow them. In the early days of the

GALLEON OF THE FIFTEENTH CENTURY.
(*Jurien de la Gravière.*)

conquest of Egypt the Khalif 'Omar wrote to his general and asked him what the sea was like, to which 'Amr made answer : " The Sea is a huge beast which silly folk ride like worms on logs ; " whereupon, much distressed, the prudent Khalif gave orders that no Moslem should voyage on so unruly an element without his leave. But it soon became clear that if the Moslems were to hold their own with their neighbours (still more if they meant to hold their neighbours' own) they must learn how to navigate ; and accordingly, in the first century of the Hijra, we find the Khalif 'Abd-el-Melik instructing his lieutenant in Africa to use Tunis as an arsenal and dockyard, and there to collect a fleet. From that time forward the Mohammedan rulers of the Barbary coast were never long without ships of some sort. The Aghlabī princes sailed forth from Tunis, and took Sicily, Sardinia, and Corsica. The Fātimī Khalifs waged war with the navies of 'Abd-er-Rahmān, the Great Khalif of Cordova, at a strength of two hundred vessels a side. The Almohades possessed a large and capacious fleet, in which they transported their armies to Spain, and their successors in North Africa, though less powerful, were generally able to keep up a number of vessels for offensive as well as commercial purposes.

During the later Middle Ages the relations between the rulers of the Barbary coast—the kings of Tunis, Tilimsān, Fez, &c.—and the trading nations of Christendom were amicable and just. Treaties show that both parties agreed in denouncing and (so

far as they could) suppressing piracy and encouraging
mutual commerce.   It was not till the beginning of
the sixteenth century that a change came over these
peaceful conditions, and the way it happened was
this.

When the united wisdom of Ferdinand and
Isabella resolved on the expatriation of the
Spanish Moors, they forgot the risk of an exile's
vengeance.[1]   No sooner was Granada fallen than
thousands of desperate Moors left the land which
for seven hundred years had been their home, and,
disdaining to live under a Spanish yoke, crossed
the strait to Africa, where they established themselves at various strong points, such as Shershēl,
Oran, and notably at Algiers, which till then had
hardly been heard of.   No sooner were the banished
Moors fairly settled in their new seats than they did
what anybody in their place would have done: they
carried the war into their oppressors' country.   To
meet the Spaniards in the open field was impossible
in their reduced numbers, but at sea their fleetness
and knowledge of the coasts gave them the opportunity of reprisal for which they longed.

Science, tradition, and observation inform us that
primitive man had certain affinities to the beast of
prey.   By superior strength or ingenuity he slew or
snared the means of subsistence.   Civilized man
leaves the coarsest forms of slaughter to a profes-
sional class, and, if he kills at all, elevates his pastime
to the rank of sport by the refining element of skill
and the excitement of uncertainty and personal risk.

[1] See S. LANE-POOLE, *The Story of the Moors in Spain*, 232–280.

But civilized man is still only too prone to prey upon his fellows, though hardly in the brutal manner of his ancestors. He preys upon inferior intelligence, upon weakness of character, upon the greed and upon the gambling instinct of mankind. In the grandest scale he is called a financier ; in the meanest, a pickpocket. This predatory spirit is at once so ancient and so general, that the reader, who is, of course, wholly innocent of such reprehensible tendencies, must nevertheless make an effort to understand the delights of robbery considered as a fine art. Some cynics there are who will tell us that the only reason we are not all thieves is because we have not pluck enough ; and there must certainly be some fascination, apart from natural depravity or original sin, to make a man prefer to run countless risks in an unlawful pursuit sooner than do an honest day's work. And in this sentence we have the answer : It is precisely the risk, the uncertainty, the danger, the sense of superior skill and ingenuity, that attract the adventurous spirit, the passion for sport, which is implanted in the vast majority of mankind.

Our Moorish robbers had all this, and more, to attract them. Brave and daring men they had shown themselves often before in their tussles with the Spaniards, or in their wild sea courses and harryings of Christian shores, in Sardinia, perhaps, or Provence ; but now they pursued a quest alluring beyond any that had gone before, a righteous vengeance upon those who had banished them from house and home, and cast them adrift to find what new anchorage they might in the world—a Holy

War against the slaughterers of their kith and kin, and the blasphemers of their sacred Faith. What joy more fierce and jubilant than to run the light brigantine down the beach of Algiers and man her for a cruise in Spanish waters? The little ship will hold but ten oars a side, each pulled by a man who knows how to fight as well as to row—as indeed he must, for there is no room for mere landsmen on board a *firkata*. But if there be a fair wind off the land, there will be little rowing ; the big lateen sail on her one mast will span the narrow waters between the African coast and the Balearic Isles, where a convenient look-out may be kept for Spanish galleons or perhaps an Italian polacca. Drawing little water, a small squadron of brigantines could be pushed up almost any creek, or lie hidden behind a rock, till the enemy hove in sight. Then oars out, and a quick stroke for a few minutes, and they are along-side their unsuspecting prey, and pouring in their first volley. Then a scramble on board, a hand-to-hand scuffle, a last desperate resistance on the poop, under the captain's canopy, and the prize is taken, the prisoners ironed, a jury crew sent on board, and all return in triumph to Algiers, where they are received with acclamations.

Or it might be a descent on the shores of their own beloved Andalusia. Then the little vessels are run into the crevices between the rocks, or even buried in the sand, and the pirates steal inland to one of the villages they know so well, and the loss of which they will never cease to mourn. They have still friends a-many in Spain, who are willing enough to help them against the oppressor and to hide them when surprised. The sleeping Spaniards are roused and then grimly silenced by the points of swords; their wives and daughters are borne away on the shoulders of the invaders; everything valuable is cleared; and

CARAVEL OF THE FIFTEENTH CENTURY.
(*Jurien de la Gravière.*)

the rovers are soon sailing merrily into the roads at Algiers, laden with spoil and captives, and often with some of the persecuted remnant of their race, who thankfully rejoin their kinsmen in the new country. To wreak such vengeance on the Spaniard added a real zest to life.

With all their skill and speed, their knowledge of the coasts, and the help of their compatriots ashore, there was still the risk of capture. Sometimes their brigantines "caught a Tartar" when they expected an easy victim, and then the Moors found the tables turned, and had to grace their captors' triumph, and for years, perhaps for ever, to sit on the banks of a Venetian or Genoese galley, heavily chained, pulling the infidel's oar even in the chase of the true believers, and gazing to satiety upon the weals which the lash kept raw on the bare back of the man in front. But the risk added a zest to the Corsair's life, and the captive could often look forward to the hope of recapture, or sometimes of ransom by his friends. The career of the pirate, with all its chances, was a prosperous one. The adventurers grew rich, and their strong places on the Barbary coast became populous and well garrisoned ; and, by the time the Spaniards began to awake to the danger of letting such troublesome neighbours alone, the evil was past a cure. For twenty years the exiled Moors had enjoyed immunity, while the big Spanish galleys were obstinately held in port, contemptuous of so small a foe. At last Don Pedro Navarro was despatched by Cardinal Ximenes to bring the pirates to book. He had little difficulty in taking possession of Oran and Bujēya ; and Algiers was so imperfectly fortified, that he imposed his own terms. He made the Algerines vow to renounce piracy ; and, to see that they kept their word, he built and garrisoned a strong fort, the "Peñon de Alger,"[1] to stop their boats from sallying forth. But the Moors had still more than one strong post on the rocky promontories of Barbary, and having tasted the delights of chasing Spaniards, they were not likely to reform, especially as the choice lay between piracy and starvation. Dig they would not, and they preferred to beg by force, like the "gentlemen of the road." So they bided their time, till Ferdinand the Catholic passed away to his account, and then, in defiance of the Peñon, and reckless of all the pains and penalties of Spanish retribution, they threw up their allegiance, and looked about for allies.

Help was not far off, though in this case it meant mastery. The day of the Moorish pirates was over; henceforth they might, and did, triumphantly assault and batter Spanish and Venetian ships, but they would do this under the captaincy of the allies they had called in, under the leadership of the Turkish Corsairs. The Moors had shown the way, and the Corsairs needed little bidding to follow it.

[1] Algiers is in Arabic, Al-Gezaïr ("the Islands"), said to be so called from that in its bay; or, more probably, Al-Gezaïr is a grammarian's explanation of the name Tzeyr or Tzier, by which the Algerians commonly called their city, and which is, I suspect, a corruption of the Roman city *Caesarea* (Augusta), which occupied almost the same site. It should be remarked that the Algerians pronounce the *gîm* hard : not Al-Jezaïr. Europeans spelt the name in all sorts of ways : Arger, Argel, Argeir, Algel, &c., down to the French Alger and our Algiers.

II.

THE LAND OF THE CORSAIRS.

IT is time to ask how it was that a spacious land seemed to lie vacant for the Corsairs to occupy, and a land too that offered almost every feature that a pirate could desire for the safe and successful prosecution of his trade. Geographers tell us that in climate and formation the island of Barbary, for such it is geologically, is really part of Europe, towards which, in history, it has played so unfriendly a part. Once the countries, which we now know as Tunis, Algiers, and Morocco, stood up abruptly as an island, with a comparatively small lake washing its northern shore, and a huge ocean on the south (see the map). That ocean is now the *Sahra* or Sáhara, which engineers dream of again flooding with salt water, and so forming an inland African sea. The lake is now the Mediterranean, or rather its western basin, for we know that the Barbary island was once nearly a peninsula, joined at its two ends to Spain and Sicily, and that its Atlas ranges formed the connection between the Sierra Nevada and Mt. Aetna. By degrees the Isthmus between Cape Bona and Sicily sank out of sight, and the ocean flowed between

Spain and Africa, while the great sea to the south
dried up into the immense stony waste which is
known preëminently as *the* Sahra, the Desert, "a tract
of land, bare as the back of a beast, without trees or
mountains."

Through one or both of these narrow straits,
Gibraltar and Malta, all vessels from the outer ocean
bound for the ports of France and Italy and the

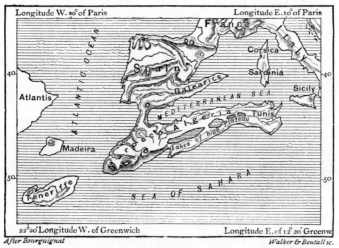

THE BARBARY PENINSULA.
(*Elisée Reclus.*)

Levant, were obliged to pass; and it must be remembered that just about the time when the Corsairs
made their appearance in Barbary, the riches of the
new-found Western world were beginning to pour
through the straits to meet those of the East, which
were brought to France and Spain, England and
Holland, from Alexandria and Smyrna.   An im-

mense proportion of the trade of Europe had to cross the western basin of the Mediterranean, of which Barbary formed the southern boundary. Any bold man who could hold Tunis at the eastern corner, or Algiers in the middle, or Ceuta or Tangiers at the western point, might reckon upon numerous opportunities of stopping argosies of untold wealth as they passed by his lair. The situation seemed purposely contrived for Corsairs.

More than this, the coast was just what a pirate wants. The map shows a series of natural harbours, often backed by lagunes which offer every facility for the escape of the rover from his pursuers ; and while in the sixteenth century there were no deep ports for vessels of heavy draught, there were endless creeks, shallow harbours, and lagunes where the Corsairs' galleys (which never drew more than six feet of water) could take refuge. Behind Jerba, the fabled island of the Lotus-Eaters, was an immense inland sea, commanded in the Middle Ages by castles, and affording a refuge for which the rovers had often had cause to be grateful. Merchant vessels were shy of sailing in the dangerous Gulf of the Greater Syrtes with its heavy tides and spreading sandbanks, and even the war-galleys of Venice and Spain were at a disadvantage when manoeuvring in its treacherous eddies against the Corsair who knew every inch of the coast. Passing westward, a famous medieval fortress, with the remains of a harbour, is seen at Mahdīya, the "Africa" of the chroniclers. Next, Tunis presents the finest harbour on all the Barbary coast ; within its Goletta (or "Throat") a vessel is

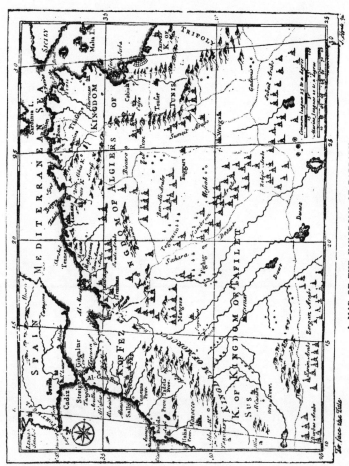

A MAP OF THE KINGDOMS OF BARBARY.

(*Voyages to Barbary for the Redemption of Captives*, 1736.)

safe from all the winds that blow, and if a canal were
cut to join it with the inland lake of Bizerta, a deep
harbour would be formed big enough to hold all the
shipping of the Mediterranean. The ancient ports of
Carthage and Porto Farina offered more protection
in the Corsairs' time than now when the sand has
choked the coast ; and in the autumn months a vessel
needed all the shelter she could get when the Cyprian
wind was blowing off Cape Bona. Close to the present Algerine frontier is Tabarka, which the Lomellini family of Genoa found a thriving situation for
their trading establishments. Lacalle, once a famous
nest of pirates, had then a fine harbour, as the merchants of Marseilles discovered when they superintended the coral fisheries from the neighbouring
Bastion de France. Bona, just beyond, has its roads,
and formerly possessed a deep harbour. Jijil, an
impregnable post, held successively by Phoenicians,
Normans, Romans, Pisans, and Genoese, till Barbarossa got possession of it and made it a fortress of
refuge for his Corsairs, stands on a rocky peninsula
joined by a sandy isthmus to the mainland, with a
port well sheltered by a natural breakwater. Further
on were Bujēya (Bougie), its harbour well protected
from the worst winds ; Algiers, not then a port, but
soon to become one ; Shershēl, with a harbour to be
shunned in a heavy swell from the north, but otherwise a valuable nook for sea rovers ; Tinnis, not always
accessible, but safe when you were inside ; and Oran,
with the important harbour of Mars El-Kebir the
" Portus Divinus " of the Romans ; while beyond, the
Jamia-el-Ghazawāt or Pirates' Mosque, shows where

a favourite creek offered an asylum between the
Brothers Rocks for distressed Corsairs.   Passing
Tangiers and Ceuta (Septa), and turning beyond the
Straits, various shelters are found, and amongst others
the celebrated ports of Salē, which, in spite of its bar
of sand, managed to send out many mischievous craft
to harass the argosies on their return from the New
World.

Not only were there ports in abundance for the
shelter of galleys, but the land behind was all that
could be desired.   River indeed there was none,
capable of navigation, but the very shortness of the
watershed which precluded the possibility of great
streams brought with it a counterbalancing advantage ; for the mountains rise so steep and high
near the coast that the Corsairs' look-out could
sight the vessels to be attacked a long way out to
sea, and thus give notice of a prize or warning of an
enemy.   Moreover the land produced all that was
needed to content the heart of man.   Below the
mountains where the Berbers dwelt and the steppes
where Arab shepherds roamed, fertile valleys spread
to the seashore.   Jerba was a perfect garden of corn
and fruit, vines, olives, almonds, apricots, and figs ;
Tunis stood in the midst of green fields, and deserved
the title of " the White, the Odoriferous, the Flowery
Bride of the West,"—though, indeed, the second epithet,
according to its inhabitants, was derived from the
odour of the lake which received the drainage of the
city, to which they ascribed its peculiar salubrity.

What more could be required in a land which was
now to become a nest of pirates ?   Yet, as though

this were not sufficient, one more virtue was added. The coast was visited by terrible gales, which, while avoidable by those who had experience and knew where to run, were fatal to the unwary, and foiled many an attack of the avenging enemy.

It remains to explain how it was that the Corsairs were able to possess themselves of this convenient territory, which was neither devoid of inhabitants nor without settled governments.

North Africa — the only Africa known to the ancients—had seen many rulers come and go since the Arabs under Okba first overran its plains and valleys. Dynasty had succeeded dynasty ; the Arab governors under the Khalifs of Damascus and Baghdad had made room for the Houses of Idrīs (A.D. 788) and Aghlab (800); these in turn had given way to the Fātimī Khalifs (909) ; and when these schismatics removed their seat of power from their newly founded capital of Mahdīya to their final metropolis of Cairo (968), their western empire speedily split up into the several princedoms of the Zeyrīs of Tunis, the Benī Hammād of Tilimsān, and other minor governments. At the close of the eleventh century, the Murābits or Almoravides, a Berber dynasty, imposed their authority over the greater part of North Africa and Spain, but gave place in the middle of the twelfth to the Muwahhids or Almohades, whose rule extended from the Atlantic to Tunis, and endured for over a hundred years. On the ruins of their vast empire three separate and long-lived dynasties sprang up : the Benī Hafs in Tunis (1228–1534), the Benī Ziyān in Central Maghrib (1235–1400), and the Benī

Merīn in Morocco (1200–1550). To complete the chronology it may be added that these were succeeded in the sixteenth century by the Corsair Pashas (afterwards Deys) of Algiers, the Turkish Pashas or Beys of Tunis, and the Sherīfs or Emperors of Morocco. The last still continue to reign; but the Deys of Algiers have given place to the French, and the Bey of Tunis is under French tutelage.

Except during the temporary excitement of a change of dynasty, the rule of these African princes was generally mild and enlightened. They came, for the most part, of the indigenous Berber population, and were not naturally disposed to intolerance or unneighbourliness. The Christians kept their churches, and were suffered to worship unmolested. We read of a Bishop of Fez as late as the thirteenth century, and the Kings of Morocco and Tunis were usually on friendly terms with the Pope. Christians were largely enrolled in the African armies, and were even appointed to civil employments. The relations of the rulers of Barbary with the European States throughout the greater part of this period—from the eleventh century, when the fighting Fātimīs left Tunis and went eastward to Egypt, to the sixteenth, when the fighting Turks came westward to molest the peace of the Mediterranean—were eminently wise and statesmanlike. The Africans wanted many of the industries of Europe; Europe required the skins and raw products of Africa: and a series of treaties involving a principle of reciprocity was the result. No doubt the naval inferiority of the African States to the trading Republics of the Mediterranean was a potent factor in bringing about this satisfactory arrangement; but it is only right to admit the remarkable fairness, moderation, and probity of the African princes in the settlement and maintenance of these treaties. As a general rule, Sicily and the commercial Republics were allied to the rulers of Tunis and Telimsān and Fez by bonds of amity and mutual advantage. One after the other, Pisa, Genoa, Provence, Aragon, and Venice, concluded commercial treaties with the African sovereigns, and renewed them from time to time. Some of these States had special quarters reserved for them at Tunis, Ceuta, and other towns; and all had their consuls in the thirteenth century, who were protected in a manner that the English agent at Algiers would have envied seventy years ago. The African trade was especially valuable to the Pisans and Genoese, and there was a regular African company trading at the Ports of Tripoli, Tunis, Bujēya, Ceuta, and Salē. Indeed, the Genoese went so far as to defend Ceuta against Christian crusaders, so much did commerce avail against religion; and, on the other hand, the Christian residents at Tunis, the western metropolis of Islam, had their own place of worship, where they were free to pray undisturbed, as late as 1530. This tolerance was largely due to the mild and judicious government of the Benī Hafs, whose three centuries' sway at Tunis was an unmixed benefit to their subjects, and to all who had relations with them.

Not that the years passed by without war and retaliation, or that treaties made piracy impossible. In the early and more pugnacious days of the

Saracen domination conflicts were frequent. The
Fātimī Khalifs conquered and held all the larger
islands of the Western Mediterranean, Sicily,
Sardinia, Corsica, and the Balearic Isles. In 1002
the Saracens pillaged Pisa, and the Pisans retaliated
by burning an African fleet. Three years later El-
Mujāhid ("Muget"), the lord of Majorca, and
conqueror of Sardinia, burnt part of Pisa; and
another incursion is recorded in 1011. From his
stronghold at Luni in Etruria this terrible scourge
ravaged the country round, until the Pope drove
him out of Italy, and the Pisans and others turned
him out of Sardinia (1017). We read of African
fleets cruising with hostile intent off the Calabrian
coast, and of the Pisans taking Bona, which was
then a nest of Corsairs (1034). Mahdīya was burnt
in 1087, and Sicily conquered by the Normans about
the same time (1072). But these were in the early
days, and even then were the exceptions; in succeeding centuries, under more settled governments, war
became very rare, and mutual amity was the prevailing
policy.[1]

Piracy was always distinctly prohibited in the
commercial treaties of the African States; nevertheless piracy went on, and most pertinaciously on the
part of the Christians. The Greeks, Sardinians,
Maltese, and Genoese were by far the worse members
of the fraternity of rovers, as the treaties themselves
prove: the increase of commerce under the stimulus
of the Crusades tempted the adventurous, and the

[1] Le Comte de Mas-Latrie, *Relations et commerce de l'Afrique
Septentrionale avec les nations chrétiennes au moyen âge*, 1886.

absence of any organized State navies gave them
immunity; and there was generally a war afoot
between some nation or other, Christian or Moslem,
and piracy (in the then state of international
law) at once became legitimate privateering. Our
buccaneers of the Spanish main had the same
apology to offer. But it is important to observe
that all this was private piracy: the African and
the Italian governments distinctly repudiated the
practice, and bound themselves to execute any
Corsair of their own country whom they might
arrest, and to deliver all his goods over to the state
which he had robbed.[1] These early Corsairs were
private freebooters, totally distinct from the authorized pirates of later days. In 1200, in time of
peace, two Pisan vessels attacked three Mohammedan
ships in Tunis roads, captured the crews, outraged
the women, and made off, vainly pursued by the
Tunisian fleet: but they received no countenance
from Pisa, the merchants of which might have
suffered severely had the Tunisians exacted reprisals. Sicily was full of Corsairs, and the King
of Tunis paid a sort of tribute to the Normans,
partly to induce them to restrain these excesses.
Aragonese and Genoese preyed upon each other
and upon the Moslems; but their doings were entirely
private and unsupported by the state.

Up to the fourteenth century the Christians were
the chief pirates of the Mediterranean, and dealt
largely in stolen goods and slaves. Then the growth

[1] LE COMTE DE MAS-LATRIE, *Relations et commerce de l'Afrique
Septentrionale avec les nations chrétiennes au moyen âge*, pp. 175-9.

of large commercial fleets discouraged the profession, and very soon we begin to hear much less of European brigandage, and much more of Moorish Corsairs. The inhabitants of the coast about the Gulf of Gabes had always shown a bent towards piracy, and the port of Mahdīya, or "Africa," now became a regular resort of sea rovers. El-Bekrī, in the twelfth century, had noticed the practice of sending galleys on the cruise for prey (perhaps during war) from the harbours of Bona ; and Ibn-Khaldūn, in the fourteenth, describes an organized company of pirates at Bujēya, who made a handsome profit from goods and the ransom of captives. The evil grew with the increase of the Turkish power in the Levant, and received a violent impetus upon the fall of Constantinople ; while on the west, the gradual expulsion of the Moors from Spain which followed upon the Christian advance filled Africa with disaffected, ruined, and vengeful Moriscos, whose one dominant passion was to wipe out their old scores with the Spaniards.

Against such influences the mild governors of North Africa were powerless. They had so long enjoyed peace and friendship with the Mediterranean States, that they were in no condition to enforce order with the strong hand. Their armies and fleets were insignificant, and their coasts were long to protect, and abounded with almost impregnable strongholds which they could not afford to garrison. Hence, when the Moors flocked over from Spain, the shores of Africa offered them a sure and accessible refuge, and the hospitable character of the Moslem's religion forbade all thought of repelling the refugees.

Still more, when the armed galleots of the Levant came crowding to Barbary, fired with the hope of rich gain, the ports were open, and the creeks afforded them shelter. A foothold once gained, the rest was easy.

It was to this land, lying ready to his use, that Captain Urūj Barbarossa came in the beginning of the sixteenth century.

PART I.

THE CORSAIR ADMIRALS.

III.

URŪJ BARBAROSSA.

1504—1515.

THE island of Lesbos has given many gifts to the world—Lesbian wine and Lesbian verse, the seven-stringed lyre, and the poems of Sappho ; but of all its products the latest was assuredly the most questionable, for the last great Lesbians were the brothers Barbarossa.

When Sultan Mohammed II. conquered the island in 1462, he left there a certain Sipāhi soldier, named Ya'kūb — so say the Turkish annalists, but the Spanish writers claim him as a native Christian— who became the father of Urūj Barbarossa and his brother Kheyr-ed-dīn. Various stories are told of their early career, and the causes which led to their taking to the sea ; but as Lesbos had long been famous for its buccaneers, whether indigenous or importations from Catalonia and Aragon, there was nothing unusual in the brothers adopting a profession which was alike congenial to bold hearts and sanctioned by time-honoured precedent.[1]   Urūj, the

---

[1] The differences between the Turkish authority, Hājji Khalīfa, who wrote in the middle of the seventeenth century and used "Memoirs"

elder, soon became the reïs, or captain, of a galleot, and finding his operations hampered in the Archipelago by the predominance of the Sultan's fleet, he determined to seek a wider and less interrupted field for his depredations. Rumours had reached the Levant of the successes of the Moorish pirates ; prodigious tales were abroad as to great argosies, laden with the treasures of the New World, passing and repassing the narrow seas between Europe and Africa, and seeming to invite capture ; and it was not long (1504) before Captain Urūj found himself cruising with two galleots off the Barbary coast, and spying out the land in search of a good harbour and a safe refuge from pursuit.

The port of Tunis offered all that a Corsair could wish. The Goletta in those days was but slightly fortified, and the principal building, besides the castle, was the custom-house, where the wealth of many nations was taxed by the Sultan of the House of Hafs. The very sight of such an institution was stimulating to a pirate. Urūj paid his court to the King of Tunis, and speedily came to an

partly inspired by Kheyr-ed-dīn himself, and the two Spanish chroniclers, Haedo and Marmol, in their narratives of the early feats and experiences of Barbarossa and his brothers, are irreconcilable in details, though the general purport is similar. Von Hammer naturally follows Hājji Khalīfa, and modern writers, like Adm. Jurien de la Gravière, take the same course. For the period of his life when Kheyr-ed-dīn was at Constantinople the Turkish writer may be reasonably preferred ; but on all matters concerning the Barbary coast the Abbot Diego de Haedo, who lived many years in Algiers in the sixteenth century, was personally acquainted with many of the servants and followers of Kheyr-ed-dīn (who died in 1546), and published his *Topographia e historia de Argel* in 1612, is undoubtedly the best informed and most trustworthy authority.

TUNIS IN THE SIXTEENTH CENTURY.
(*Sphère des deux Mondes*, 1555.)

understanding with him on the subject of royalties on stolen goods. The ports of Tunis were made free to the Corsair, and the king would protect him from pursuit, for the consideration of a fixed share—a fifth—of the booty The policy of the enlightened rulers of Tunis evidently no longer suited their latest representative.

The base of operations thus secured, Urūj did not keep his new ally long waiting for a proof of his prowess. One day he lay off the island of Elba, when two galleys-royal, belonging to his Holiness Pope Julius II., richly laden with goods from Genoa, and bound for Cività Vecchia, hove in sight. They were rowing in an easy, leisurely manner, little dreaming of Turkish Corsairs, for none such had ever been seen in those waters, nor anything bigger than a Moorish brigantine, of which the Papal marines were prepared to give a good account. So the two galleys paddled on, some ten leagues asunder, and Urūj Reïs marked his prey down. It was no light adventure for a galleot of eighteen banks of oars to board a royal galley of perhaps twice her size, and with no one could tell how many armed men inside her. The Turkish crew remonstrated at such foolhardiness, and begged their captain to look for a foe of their own size : but for reply Urūj only cast most of the oars overboard, and thus made escape impossible. Then he lay to and awaited the foremost galley. She came on, proudly, unconscious of danger. Suddenly her look-out spied Turkish turbans—a strange sight on the Italian coast—and in a panic of confusion her company beat to arms. The vessels were now along-

side, and a smart volley of shot and bolts completed
the consternation of the Christians. Urūj and his
men were quickly on the poop, and his Holiness's
servants were soon safe under hatches.

Never before had a galley-royal struck her colours
to a mere galleot. But worse was to follow. Urūj
declared he must and would have her consort. In
vain his officers showed him how temerarious was
the venture, and how much more prudent it would be
to make off with one rich prize than to court capture
by overgreediness. The Corsair's will was of iron,
and his crew, inflated with triumph, caught his
audacious spirit. They clothed themselves in the
dresses of the Christian prisoners, and manned the
subdued galley as though they were her own seamen.
On came the consort, utterly ignorant of what had
happened, till a shower of arrows and small shot
aroused her, just in time to be carried by assault,
before her men had collected their senses.

Urūj brought his prizes into the Goletta. Never
was such a sight seen there before. " The wonder and
astonishment," says Haedo,[1] " that this noble exploit
caused in Tunis, and even in Christendom, is not to
be expressed, nor how celebrated the name of Urūj
Reïs was become from that very moment ; he being
held and accounted by all the world as a most
valiant and enterprizing commander. And by reason
his beard was extremely red, or carroty, from thence-
forwards he was generally called Barba-rossa, which
in Italian signifies Red-Beard." [2]

[1] Quoted by MORGAN, *Hist. of Algiers*, 225.
[2] It is possible that Barba-rossa is but a European corruption of

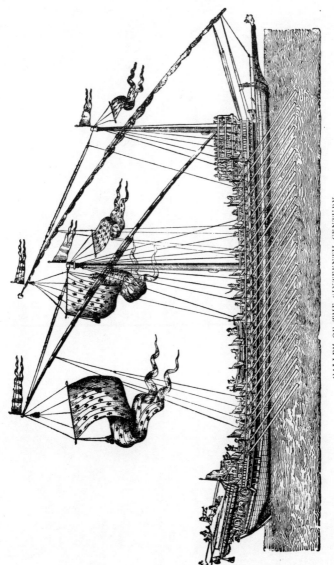

GALLEY OF THE SIXTEENTH CENTURY.

(*Jurien de la Gravière.*)

The capture of the Papal galleys gave Urūj what he wanted—rowers. He kept his Turks for fighting, and made the Christian prisoners work the oars : such was the custom of every Corsair down to the present century, and the Christian navies were similarly propelled by Mohammedan slaves. The practice must have lent a strange excitement to the battle ; for then, assuredly, a man's foes were of his own household. A Venetian admiral knew well that his two or three hundred galley slaves were panting to break their irons and join the enemy ; and the Turkish Corsair had also his unwilling subjects, who would take the first chance to mutiny in favour of the Christian adversary. Thus it often happened that a victory was secured by the strong arms of the enemy's chained partizans, who would have given half their lives to promote a defeat. But the sharp lash of the boatswain, who walked the bridge between the banks of rowers, was a present and acute argument which few backs could withstand.

Urūj had made his first *coup*, and he did not hesitate to follow it up. Next year he captured a Spanish ship with five hundred soldiers on board, who were all so sea-sick, or spent with pumping out the leaky vessel, that they fell an easy prey to his galleots. Before five years were out, what with cruising, and building with the timber of his many prizes, he had eight good vessels at his back,

Baba Urūj, "Father Urūj," as his men called him. At all events Urūj is the real Barbarossa, though modern writers generally give the name to his younger brother Kheyr-ed-dīn, who was only called Barbarossa on account of his kinship to the original.

with two of his brothers to help. The port of Tunis
now hardly sufficed his wants, so he established himself temporarily on the fertile island of Jerba, and
from its ample anchorage his ships issued forth to
harry the coasts of Italy.

To be king of Jerba was all too small a title for his
ambition. He aimed at sovereignty on a large scale,
and, Corsair as he was by nature, he wished for
settled power almost as much as he delighted
in adventure. In 1512 the opportunity he sought
arrived. Three years before, the Mohammedan King
of Bujēya had been driven out of his city by the
Spaniards, and the exiled potentate appealed to the
Corsair to come and restore him, coupling the petition
with promises of the free use of Bujēya port, whence
the command of the Spanish sea was easily to be
held. Urūj was pleased with the prospect, and as he
had now twelve galleots with cannon, and one thousand
Turkish men-at-arms, to say nothing of renegades
and Moors, he felt strong enough for the attempt.
The renown of his exploits had spread far and wide,
and there was no lack of a following from all parts of
the Levant when it was known that Urūj Reïs was
on the war-path. His extraordinary energy and
impetuosity called forth a corresponding zeal in his
men, and, like other dashing commanders, he was
very popular.

Well supported, and provided with such a siege-
train as the times permitted, he landed before Bujēya
in August, 1512, and found the dethroned king expecting him at the head of three thousand mountain
Berbers. The Spanish garrison was collected in the

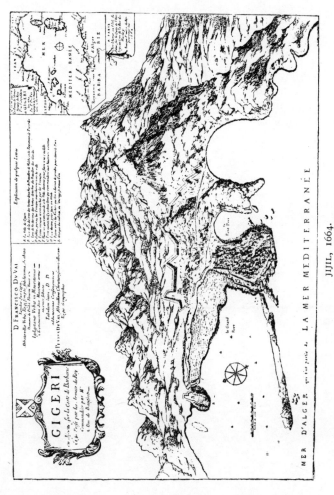

JIJIL, 1664.

(From a Map in the British Museum.)

strong bastion, which the Count Don Pedro Navarro
had fortified when he took the city, and for eight days
the fortress withstood the battering of the Corsair's
ordnance. Just when a breach began to be opened,
Urūj was disabled ; a shot took his left arm away
above the elbow. In the absence of their leader's
heroic example, the Turks felt little confidence in
their superiority to Spanish steel ; they preferred
carrying their wounded captain to the surgeons at
Tunis. Bujēya for the moment escaped, but the
Corsairs enjoyed some little consolation in the
capture of a rich Genoese galleot which they met
on its voyage to the Lomellini's mart at Tabarka.
With this spoil Urūj returned to recover from his
wound, while his brother, Kheyr-ed-dīn, kept guard
over the castle of the Goletta, and began to bring the
galleots and prizes through the canal into the Lake
of Tunis, where they would be safe from pursuit.

He was too late, however. The Senate of Genoa
was highly incensed at the loss of the galleot, and
Andrea Doria, soon to be known as the greatest
Christian admiral of his time, was despatched with
twelve galleys to exact reparation. He landed before
the Goletta, and drove Kheyr-ed-dīn before him into
Tunis. The fortress was sacked, and half Barba-
rossa's ships were brought in triumph to Genoa.
Thus ended the first meeting between Doria and
Kheyr-ed-dīn : the next was less happy for the noble
Genoese.

Kheyr-ed-dīn, well aware of his brother's fierce
humour, did not dare to face him after this humiliation, but left him to fume impotently in his sick-

room, while he stole away to Jerba, there to work night and day at shipbuilding. Urūj joined him in the following spring—the King of Tunis had probably had enough of him—and they soon had the means of wiping out their disgrace. The attempt was at first a failure ; a second assault on the ominous forts of Bujēya (1514) was on the point of success, when reinforcements arrived from Spain. The Berber allies evinced more interest in getting in their crops after the rain than in forcing the bastion ; and Barba· rossa, compelled to raise the siege, in a frantic rage, tearing his red beard like a madman, set fire to his ships that they might not fall into the hands of the Spaniards.

He would not show himself now in Tunis or Jerba. Some new spot must shelter him after this fresh reverse. On his way to and from Bujēya he had noticed the very place for his purpose—a spot easy to defend, perched on inaccessible rocks, yet furnished with a good harbour, where the losses of recent years might be repaired. This was Jījil, some sixty miles to the east of Bujēya ; whose sturdy inhabitants owed allegiance to no Sultan, but were proud to welcome so renowned, although now so unfortunate, a warrior as Barbarossa. So at Jījil Urūj dwelt, and cultivated the good-will of the people with spoils of corn and goods from his cruisers, till those "indomitable African mountaineers," who had never owned a superior, chose him by acclamation their king.

IV.

THE TAKING OF ALGIERS.

1516—1518.

THE new Sultan of Jijil was now called to a much more serious enterprize than heading his truculent highlanders against a neighbouring tribe—though it must be admitted that he was always in his element when fisticuffs were in request. An appeal had come from Algiers. The Moors there had endured for seven years the embargo of the Spaniards; they had seen their *fregatas* rotting before their eyes, and never dared to mend them; they had viewed many a rich prize sail by, and never so much as ventured a mile out to sea to look her over: for there were keen eyes and straight shots in the Peñon which commanded the bay, and King Ferdinand the Catholic held a firm hand over the tribute which his banished subjects had to pay him for his condescension in ruining them. Their occupation was gone; they had not dragged a prize ashore for years; they must rebel or starve. At this juncture Ferdinand opportunely died (1516), and the Algerine Moors seized their chance. They stopped the tribute, and called in the aid of Salim, the neighbouring Arab sheykh, whose clansmen would make the city safe on the land side. " But what are they to do with the two hundred petulant and vexatious Spaniards in the fort, who incessantly pepper the town with their cannon, and make the houses too hot to hold them ; especially when they are hungry ? Little would the gallant Arab cavalry, with their fine Libyan mares and horses, rich coats-of-mail, tough targets, well-tempered sabres, and long supple lances, avail them against the Spanish volleys. And who so proper to redress this grievance as the invincible Barbarossa, who was master of a naval force, and wanted not artillery ? Had he not been twice to reinstate the unfortunate King of Bujēya, and lost a limb in his service ?

" Without the least deliberation Prince Salim despatched a solemn embassy to Jījil, intreating Barbarossa, in whom he and his people reposed their entire confidence, to hasten to their assistance. No message whatever could have been more welcome to the ambitious Barbarossa than one of this nature. His new-acquired realm brought him in but a very scanty revenue ; nor was he absolute. . . . He had been wretchedly baffled at Bujēya, but hoped for better success at Algiers, which, likewise, is a place of much greater consequence, and much more convenient for his purpose, which, as has been said, was to erect a great monarchy of his own in Barbary." [1]

With some six thousand men and sixteen galleots Urūj set forth by sea and land to the rescue of Algiers. First he surprised Shershēl, a strong position

[1] MORGAN, *Hist. of Algiers*, 233. (1731.)

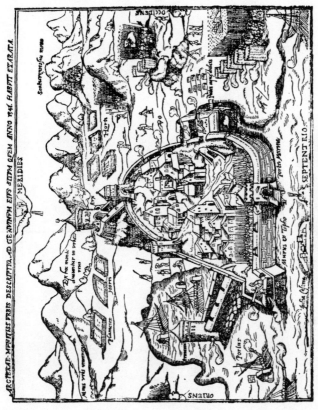

ALGIERS IN THE SIXTEENTH CENTURY.
(*Sphère des deux Mondes*, 1555.)

fifteen leagues to the west of Algiers, which had been
occupied by Moors from Granada, and was now commanded by a bold Turkish Corsair, Kara Hasan,
who, emulating his old comrade's success with the
people of Jījil, had induced the Shershēl rovers to
accept him as their leader. Urūj had no liking for
two Kings of Brentford, and took off Black Hasan's
head as a friendly precaution, before exposing himself
to the perils of another contest with the Spaniards.

Soon he was at Algiers, hospitably lodged and
entertained, he and all his men, Turks and Jījilis
alike, by Sheykh Salim and the people of the town.
There, at the distance of a crossbow-shot, stood the
fortress he had come to reduce, and thither he sent a
message offering a safe conduct to the garrison if
they would surrender The Spanish captain made
reply that "neither threats nor proffered curtesies
availed aught with men of his kidney," and told him
to remember Bujēya. Upon which Urūj, more to
please his unsuspicious hosts than with much prospect
of success, battered the Peñon for twenty days with
his light field-pieces, without making any sensible
breach in the defences.

Meanwhile, the Arabs and Moors who had called
him to their aid were becoming aware of their
mistake. Instead of getting rid of their old enemy
the Spaniard, they had imported a second, worse than
the first, and Urūj soon showed them who was to be
master. He and his Turks treated the ancient
Moorish families, who had welcomed them within
their gates, with an insolence that was hard to be
borne by descendants of the Abencerrages and other

5

noble houses of Granada.   Salim, the Arab Sheykh,
was the first to feel the despot's power: he was
murdered in his bath—it was said by the Corsair
himself.   In their alarm, the Algerines secretly made
common cause with the soldiers of the Peñon, and a
general rising was planned ; but one day at Friday
prayers Barbarossa let the crowded congregation
know that their designs were not unsuspected.
Shutting the gates, the Turks bound their enter-
tainers with the turbans off their heads, and the
immediate decapitation of the ringleaders at the
mosque door quelled the spirit of revolt.   Nor was a
great Armada, sent by Cardinal Ximenes, and commanded by Don Diego de Vera, more successful than
the Algerine rebellion.   Seven thousand Spaniards
were utterly routed by the Turks and Arabs ; and to
complete the discomfiture of the Christians a violent
tempest drove their ships ashore, insomuch that this
mighty expedition was all but annihilate.

An adventurer who, with a motley following of
untrained bandits and nomads, could overthrow a
Spanish army was a phenomenon which the Christian
States now began to eye with considerable anxiety.
From the possessor of a strong place or two on the
coast, he had become nothing less than the Sultan of
Middle Barbary (*Maghrib el-Awsat*). When the Prince
of Tinnis raised the whole country side against him,
and a mighty host was rolling down upon Algiers,
Urūj marched out with one thousand Turks and
five hundred Moors, and never a cannon amongst
them, and smote the enemy hip and thigh, and
pursued them into their own city.   The prince of

Tinnis took to the mountains, and Urūj Barbarossa
reigned in his stead (1517). Then Tilimsān
fell into his possession, and save that the Spaniards
held Oran and two or three fortresses, such as
the Peñon de Alger and Bujēya, his dominions
coincided with modern Algeria, and marched with
the kingdoms of Tunis and Fez. He was in a
position to form alliances with Fez and Morocco.
His galleots were punctilious, moreover, in returning
the call of Don Diego de Vera, and many an
expectant merchant in Genoa, or Naples, or Venice,
strained his eyes in vain for the argosy that, thanks
to the Corsair's vigilance, would never again sail
proudly into the harbour.

When all this came to the ears of the new King of
Spain, afterwards the Emperor Charles V., he yielded
to the prayer of the Marquis de Comares, Governor of
Oran, and despatched ten thousand veterans to make
an end of the Corsairs once and for ever. Urūj Barbarossa was then stationed at Tilimsān with only 1,500
men, and when the hosts of the enemy drew near he
made a bolt by night for Algiers, taking his Turks and
his treasure with him. The news soon reached the
enemy's scouts, and the Marquis gave hot pursuit. A
river with steep banks lay in the fugitives' path : could
they pass it, they would have the chances in their
favour. Urūj scattered his jewels and gold behind him,
vainly hoping to delay the greedy Spaniards ; but
Comares trampled over everything, and came up with
the Turkish rear when but half their force had crossed
the river. Their leader was already safe on the other
side, but the cries of his rear-guard brought him back.

The Corsair was not the man to desert his followers, and without an instant's hesitation he recrossed the fatal stream and threw himself into the fray. Hardly a Turk or a Moor escaped from that bloody field. Facing round, they fought till they dropped; and among them the vigorous figure of Barbarossa was ever to be seen, laying about him with his one arm like a lion to the last.

" Urūj Barbarossa, according to the testimony of those who remember him, was, when he died, about forty-four years of age. He was not very tall of stature, but extremely well set and robust. His hair and beard perfectly red; his eyes quick, sparkling and lively; his nose aquiline or Roman; and his complexion between brown and fair. He was a man excessively bold, resolute, daring, magnanimous, enterprizing, profusely liberal, and in nowise bloodthirsty, except in the heat of battle, nor rigorously cruel but when disobeyed. He was highly beloved, feared, and respected, by his soldiers and domestics, and when dead was by them all in general most bitterly regretted and lamented. He left neither son nor daughter. He resided in Barbary fourteen years, during which the harms he did to the Christians are inexpressible." [1]

[1] MORGAN, 257.

V.

KHEYR-ED-DIN BARBAROSSA.

1518—1530.

URŪJ BARBAROSSA, the gallant, impulsive, reckless, lovable soldier of fortune was dead, and it seemed as if all the power he had built up by his indomitable energy must inevitably vanish with its founder. The Marquis de Comares and the Spanish army held the fate of Algiers in their hands ; one steady march, and surely the Corsairs must be swept out of Africa. But, with what would seem incredible folly, if it had not been often repeated, the troops were shipped back to Spain, the Marquis returned to his post at Oran, and the opportunity was lost for three hundred years. The Algerines drew breath again, and their leader began to prepare fresh schemes of conquest.

The mantle of Urūj had fallen upon worthy shoulders. The elder brother possessed, indeed, matchless qualities for deeds of derring-do ; to lead a storming party, board a galleon,—cut and thrust and "have at you,"—he had no equal : but Kheyr-ed-dīn, with like courage and determination, was gifted with prudent and statesmanlike intelligence, which led him

to greater enterprizes, though not to more daring
exploits. He measured the risk by the end, and
never exposed himself needlessly to the hazard of
defeat : but when he saw his way clear, none struck
harder or more effectual blows.[1]

His first proceeding was typical of his sagacious
mind. He sent an ambassador to Constantinople, to
lay his homage at the feet of the Grand Signior, and
to beg his Majesty's favour and protection for the
new province of Algiers, which was now by his humble
servant added to the Ottoman Empire. The reply
was gracious. Selīm had just conquered Egypt, and
Algiers formed an important western extension of his
African dominion. The sage Corsair was immediately
appointed Beglerbeg, or Governor-General, of Algiers
(1519), and invested with the insignia of office, the
horse and scimitar and horsetail-banner. Not only
this, but the Sultan sent a guard of two thousand
Janissaries to his viceroy's aid, and offered special
inducements to such of his subjects as would pass
westward to Algiers and help to strengthen the
Corsair's authority.

The Beglerbeg lost no time in repairing the damage
of the Spaniards. He reinforced his garrisons along
the coast, at Meliana, Shershēl, Tinnis, and Musta-

---

[1] Kheyr-ed-dīn (pronounced by the Turks *Hare-udeen*), as has been
said, is the Barbarossa of modern writers, and it is probable that the
name was given to him originally under some impression that it was of
the nature of a family name. Haedo, Marmol, and Hājji Khalīfa all
give him this title, though his beard was auburn, while Urūj was the
true " Red-Beard." Neither of the brothers was ever called Barbarossa
by Turks or Moors, and Hājji Khalīfa records the title merely as used
by Europeans. The popular usage is here adopted.

ghānim, and struck up alliances with the great Arab
tribes of the interior. An armada of some fifty men-
of-war and transports, including eight galleys-royal,
under the command of Admiral Don Hugo de Mon-
cada, in vain landed an army of veterans on the
Algerine strand : they were driven back in confusion,
and one of those storms, for which the coast bears so

OBSERVATION WITH THE CROSSBOW.
(*Jurien de la Gravière.*)

evil a name, finished the work of Turkish steel (1519).
One after the other, the ports and strongholds of
Middle Barbary fell into the Corsair's hands: Col,
Bona, Constantine, owned the sway of Kheyr-ed-dīn
Barbarossa, who was now free to resume his favourite
occupation of scouring the seas in search of Christian
quarry. Once or twice in every year he would lead

out his own eighteen stout galleots, and call to his side
other daring spirits whom the renown of his name had
drawn from the Levant, each with his own swift
cruiser manned by stout arms and the pick of Turkish
desperadoes.   There you might see him surrounded
by captains who were soon to be famous wherever
ships were to be seized or coasts harried ;—by Dragut,
Sālih Reïs, Sinān the "Jew of Smyrna," who was
suspected of black arts because he could take a
declination with the crossbow, and that redoubtable
rover Aydin Reïs, whom the Spaniards dubbed *Cacha-
diablo*, or "Drub-devil," though he had better been
named Drub-Spaniard.   The season for cruising began
in May, and lasted till the autumn storms warned
vessels to keep the harbours, or at least to attempt no
distant expeditions.   During the summer months the
Algerine galleots infested every part of the Western
Mediterranean, levied contributions of slaves and
treasure upon the Balearic Isles and the coasts of
Spain, and even passed beyond the straits to waylay
the argosies which were returning to Cadiz laden with
the gold and jewels of the Indies.   Nothing was safe
from their attacks ; not a vessel ran the gauntlet of
the Barbary coast in her passage from Spain to Italy
without many a heart quaking within her.   The
"Scourge of Christendom" had begun, which was to
keep all the nations of Europe in perpetual alarm for
three centuries.   The Algerine Corsairs were masters
of the sea, and they made their mastery felt by all who
dared to cross their path ; and not merchantmen only,
but galleys-royal of his Catholic Majesty learnt to
dread the creak of the Turkish rowlock.

One day in 1529 Kheyr-ed-dīn despatched his trusty lieutenant "Drub-Devil" with fourteen galleots to make a descent upon Majorca and the neighbouring islands. No job could be more suited to the Corsair's taste, and Sālih Reïs, who was with him, fully shared his enjoyment of the task. The pair began in the usual way by taking several prizes on the high seas, dropping down upon the islands and the Spanish coasts, and carrying off abundance of Christians to serve at the oar, or to purchase their liberty with those pieces-of-eight which never came amiss to the rover's pockets. Tidings reaching them of a party of Moriscos who were eager to make their escape from their Spanish masters, and were ready to pay handsomely for a passage to Barbary. "Drub-Devil" and his comrades landed by night near Oliva, embarked two hundred families and much treasure, and lay-to under the island of Formentara. Unfortunately General Portundo, with eight Spanish galleys, was just then on his way back from Genoa, whither he had conveyed Charles V. to be crowned Emperor by the Pope at Bologna ; and, being straightway informed of the piratical exploit which had taken place, bore away for the Balearic Isles in hot pursuit. "Drub-Devil" hastily landed his Morisco friends, to be the better prepared to fight or run, for the sight of eight big galleys was more than he had bargained for ; but to his surprise the enemy came on, well within gunshot, without firing a single round. Portundo was anxious not to sink the Turks, for fear of drowning the fugitive Moriscos, whom he supposed to be on board, and for whose recapture he was to have ten thousand ducats ; but the Corsairs imputed his conduct to cowardice, and, suddenly changing their part from attacked to attackers, they swooped like eagles upon the galleys, and after a brisk hand-to-hand combat, in which Portundo was slain, they carried seven of them by assault, and sent the other flying at topmost speed to Iviça. This bold stroke brought to Algiers, besides the Moriscos, who had watched the battle anxiously from the island, many valuable captives of rank, and released hundreds of Moslem galley-slaves from irons and the lash.[1] "Drub-Devil" had a splendid reception, we may be sure, when the people of Algiers saw seven royal galleys, including the *capitana*, or flagship, of Spain, moored in their roads ; and it is no wonder that with such triumphs the new Barbary State flourished exceedingly.

Fortified by a series of unbroken successes, Kheyr-ed-dīn at last ventured to attack the Spanish garrison, which had all this time affronted him at the Peñon de Alger. It was provoking to be obliged to beach his galleots a mile to the west, and to drag them painfully up the strand ; and the merchantmen, moored east of the city, were exposed to the weather to such a degree as to imperil their commerce. Kheyr-ed-dīn resolved to have a port of his own at Algiers, with no Spanish bridle to curb him. He summoned Don Martin de Vargas to surrender, and, on his refusal, bombarded the Peñon day and night for fifteen days with heavy cannon, partly founded in Algiers, partly seized from a French

[1] MORGAN, 264-6.

galleon, till an assault was practicable, when the
feeble remnant of the garrison was quickly over-
powered and sent to the bagnios. The stones of
the fortress were used to build the great mole which
protects Algiers harbour on the west, and for two
whole years the Christian slaves were laboriously
employed upon the work.

To aggravate this disaster, a curious sight was
seen a fortnight after the fall of the Peñon. Nine
transports, full of men and ammunition for the
reinforcement of the garrison, hove in sight, and
long they searched to and fro for the well-known
fortress they had come to succour. And whilst
they marvelled that they could not discover it, out
dashed the Corsairs in their galleots and light
shebēks, and seized the whole convoy, together
with two thousand seven hundred captives and a fine
store of arms and provisions.[1]

Everything that Kheyr-ed-dīn took in hand seemed
to prosper. His fleet increased month by month, till
he had thirty-six of his own galleots perpetually on
the cruise in the summer season ; his prizes were
innumerable, and his forces were increased by the
fighting men of the seventy thousand Moriscos whom
he rescued, in a series of voyages, from servitude in
Spain. The waste places of Africa were peopled
with the industrious agriculturists and artisans whom
the Spanish Government knew not how to employ.
The foundries and dockyards of Algiers teemed
with busy workmen. Seven thousand Christian

[1] JURIEN DE LA GRAVIÈRE, *Doria et Barberousse*, Pt. I.,
ch. xxi.

slaves laboured at the defensive works and the
harbour ; and every attempt of the Emperor to
rescue them and destroy the pirates was repelled
with disastrous loss.

VI

1470—1522.

NO one appreciated better the triumphs of the Beglerbeg of Algiers than Sultan Suleymān. The Ottomans, as yet inexperienced in naval affairs, were eager to take lessons. The Turkish navy had been of slow growth, chiefly because in early days there were always people ready to act as sailors for pay. When Murād I. wished to cross from Asia to Europe to meet the invading army of Vladislaus and Hunyady, the Genoese skippers were happy to carry over his men for a ducat a head, just to spite their immemorial foes the Venetians, who were enlisted on the other side. It was not till the fall of Constantinople gave the Turks the command of the Bosphorus that Mohammed II. resolved to create for himself a naval power.

That fatal jealousy between the Christian States which so often aided the progress of the Turks helped them now. The great commercial republics, Genoa and Venice, had long been struggling for supremacy on the sea. Venice held many important posts among the islands of the Archipelago and on the Syrian coast, where the Crusaders had rewarded her naval assistance with the gift of the fortress of Acre. Genoa was stronger in the Black Sea and Marmora, where, until the coming of the Turks, her colony at Galata was little less than an Oriental Genoa. The Genoese tower is still seen on the steep slope of Pera, and Genoese forts are common objects in the Bosphorus, and in the Crimea, where they dominate the little harbour of Balaklava. The Sea of Marmora was the scene of many a deadly contest between the rival fleets. In 1352, under the walls of Constantinople, the Genoese defeated the combined squadrons of the Venetians, the Catalonians, and the Greeks. But next year the Bride of the Sea humbled the pride of Genoa in a disastrous engagement off Alghero; and in 1380, when the Genoese had gained possession of Chioggia and all but occupied Venice itself, the citizens rose like one man to meet the desperate emergency, and not only repulsed, but surrounded the invaders, and forced them to capitulate. From this time Genoa declined in power, while Venice waxed stronger and more haughty. The conquest of Constantinople by the Turks, followed rapidly by the expulsion of the Genoese from Trebizond, Sinope, Kaffa, and Azov, was the end of the commercial prosperity of the Ligurian Republic in the East. The Black Sea and Marmora were now Turkish lakes. The Castles of the Dardanelles, mounted with heavy guns, protected any Ottoman fleet from pursuit; and though Giacomo Veniero defiantly carried his own ship

AN ADMIRAL'S GALLEY.

(*Furttenbach, Architectura Navalis,* 1629.)

Derck Josga Radermach

under fire through the strait and back again with
the loss of only eleven men, no one cared to follow
his example.

When Mohammed II. issued forth with a fleet of
one hundred galleys and two hundred transports,
carrying seventy thousand troops, and ravished the
Negropont away from Venice in 1470, he had only
to repass the Hellespont to be absolutely safe. All
that the Venetian admirals, the famous Loredani,
could do was to retaliate upon such islands of the
Archipelago as were under Turkish sway and ravage
the coasts of Asia Minor. Superior as they were to
the Turks in the building and management of galleys,
they had not the military resources of their foe.
Their troops were mercenaries, not to be compared
with the Janissaries and Sipāhis, though the hardy
Stradiotes from Epirus, dressed like Turks, but
without the turban, of whom Othello is a familiar
specimen, came near to rivalling them. On land,
the Republic could not meet the troops of the
Grand Signior, and after her very existence had
been menaced by the near approach of a Turkish
army on the banks of the Piave[1] (1477), Venice
made peace, and even, it is said, incited the Turks
to the capture of Otranto. The Ottoman galleys
were now free of the Adriatic, and carried fire and
sword along the Italian coast, insomuch that whenever the crescent was seen at a vessel's peak the
terrified villagers fled inland, and left their homes
at the mercy of the pirates. The period of the
Turkish Corsairs had already begun.

See S. LANE-POOLE, *The Story of Turkey*, 135.

There was another naval power to be reckoned with besides discredited Genoa and tributary Venice. The Knights Hospitallers of Jerusalem, driven from Smyrna (in 1403) by Timur, had settled at Rhodes, which they hastened to render impregnable. Apparently they succeeded, for attack after attack from the Mamlūk Sultans of Egypt failed to shake them from their stronghold, whence they commanded the line of commerce between Alexandria and Constantinople, and did a brisk trade in piracy upon passing vessels. The Knights of Rhodes were the Christian Corsairs of the Levant ; the forests of Caramania furnished them with ships, and the populations of Asia Minor supplied them with slaves. So long as they roved the seas the Sultan's galleys were ill at ease. Even Christian ships suffered from their high-handed proceedings, and Venice looked on with open satisfaction when, in 1480, Mohammed II. despatched one hundred and sixty ships and a large army to humble the pride of the Knights. The siege failed, however ; D'Aubusson, the Grand Master, repulsed the general assault with furious heroism, and the Turks retired with heavy loss.[1]

Finding that the Ottomans were not quite invincible, Venice plucked up heart, and began to prepare for hostilities with her temporary ally. The interval of friendliness had been turned to good account by the Turks. Yāni, the Christian shipbuilder of the Sultan, had studied the improvements of the Venetians, and he now constructed two immense *kokas*, seventy cubits long and thirty in the beam, with

[1] See *The Story of Turkey*, 136.

masts of several trees spliced together, measuring four cubits round. Forty men in armour might stand in the maintop and fire down upon the enemy. There were two decks, one like a galleon's deck, and the other like a galley, each with a big gun on either side. Four-and-twenty oars a side, on the upper deck, were propelled each by nine men. Boats hung from the stern ; and the ship's complement consisted (so says Hājji Khalīfa)[1] of two thousand soldiers and sailors. Kemāl Reïs and Borāk Reïs commanded these two prodigies, and the whole fleet, numbering some three hundred other vessels, was despatched to the Adriatic under the command of Daūd Pasha. The object of attack was Lepanto.

Towards the end of July, 1499, they sighted the Venetian fleet, which was on the look-out for them, off Modon. They counted forty-four galleys, sixteen galleasses, and twenty-eight ordinary sail. Neither courted an action, which each knew to be fraught with momentous consequences. Grimani, the Venetian admiral, retired to Navarino ; the Turks anchored off Sapienza. On August 12th Daūd Pasha, who knew the Sultan was awaiting him with the land forces at Lepanto, resolved to push on at all costs. In those days Turkish navigators had little confidence in the open sea , they preferred to hug the shore, where they might run into a port in case of bad weather. Daūd accordingly endeavoured to pass between the island of Prodano and the Morea, just north of Navarino. Perfectly aware of his course, the Venetians had drawn out their fleet

---

[1] *History of the Maritime Wars of the Turks*, 20.

at the upper end of the narrow passage, where they had the best possible chance of catching the enemy in confused order. The Proveditore of Corfu, Andrea Loredano, had reinforced the Christian fleet that very day with ten ships ; the position was well chosen ; the wind was fair, and drove full down upon the Turks as they emerged from the strait. But the Venetian admiral placed his chief reliance in his galleasses, and as yet the art of manoeuvring sailing vessels in battle array was in its youth. Bad steering here, a wrong tack there, and then ship ran against ship, the great galleasses became entangled and helpless, carried by the wind into the midst of the enemy, or borne away where they were useless, and the Turkish galleys had it all their own way. Loredano's flagship burnt down to the water, and other vessels were destroyed by fire. Yāni's big ships layed an important part in the action. Two galleasses, each containing a thousand men, and two other vessels, surrounded Borāk Reïs, but the smaller ships could not fire over the *koka's* lofty sides, and were speedily sunk. Borāk Reïs threw burning pitch into the galleasses, and burnt up crews and ships, till, his own vessel catching fire, he and other notable captains, after performing prodigies of valour, perished in the flames. Wherefore the island of Prodano is by the Turks called Borāk Isle to this day.[1] To the Christians the action was known as " the deplorable battle of Zonchio," from the name of the old castle of Navarino, beneath which it was fought.

[1] Hājji Khalifa, 21.

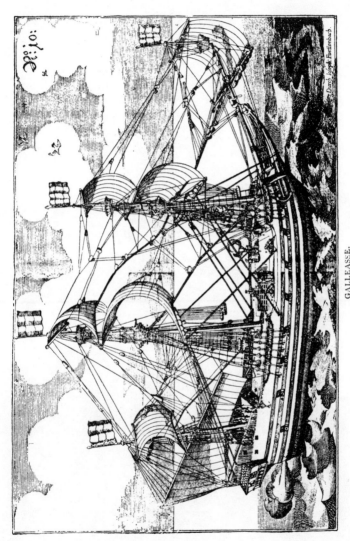

GALLEASSE.

(*Furttenbach, Architectura Navalis,* 1629.)

In spite of his success at Zonchio, Daūd Pasha had still to fight his way up to Lepanto. The Venetians had collected their scattered fleet, and had been reinforced by their allies of France and Rhodes ; it was clear they were bent on revenge. The Turks hugged the land, dropped anchor at night, and kept a sharp look-out. It was a perpetual skirmish all the way. The Venetians tried to surprise the enemy at their moorings, but they were already at sea, and squally weather upset Grimani's strategy and he had the mortification of seeing his six fire-ships burning innocuously with never a Turk the worse. Again and again it seemed impossible that Daūd could escape, but Grimani's Fabian policy delivered the enemy out of his hands, and when finally the Turkish fleet sailed triumphantly into the Gulf of Patras, where it was protected by the Sultan's artillery at Lepanto, the Grand Prior of Auvergne, who commanded the French squadron, sailed away in disgust at the pusillanimity of his colleague. Lepanto fell, August 28th ; and Grimani was imprisoned, nominally for life. for his blundering : nevertheless, after twenty-one years he was made Doge.[1]

Venice never recovered from her defeat. The loss of Lepanto and the consequent closing of the gulfs of Patras and Corinth were followed by the capture of Modon, commanding the strait of Sapienza : the east coast of the Adriatic and Ionian seas was no longer open to Christian vessels. The Oriental trade of the republic was further seriously impaired by the Turkish

[1] JURIEN DE LA GRAVIÈRE, *Doria et Barberousse*, Pt. I., ch. xv.

conquest of Egypt (1517),[1] which deprived her of her most important mart; and the discovery of the New World brought Spanish traders into successful competition with her own. Venice indeed was practically an Oriental city; her skilled workmen learned their arts in Egypt and Mesopotamia; her bazaars were filled with the products of the East, with the dimity and other cloths and silks and brocades of Damietta, Alexandria, Tinnēs, and Cairo, cotton from Ba'lbekk, silk from Baghdād, atlas satin from Ma'din in Armenia; and she introduced to Europe not only the products of the East, but their very names. Sarcenet is Saracen stuff; tabby is named after a street in Baghdād where watered silk was made; Baldacchini are simply "Baldac," *i.e.*, Baghdād, canopies; samite is Shāmī, "Syrian," fabric; the very coat of the Egyptian, the *jubba*, is preserved in giuppa, jupe.[2] With the loss of her Oriental commerce, which the hostility of the Turks involved, Venice could no longer hold her own. She bowed to her fate and acknowledged the Turkish supremacy by sea as well as by land. She even paid the Sultan tribute for the island of Cyprus. When Suleymān the Magnificent succeeded Selīm and took Belgrade (1521), Venice hastily increased her payment and did homage for Zante as well. So meek had now become the Bride of the Sea.

Turkey still suffered the annoyance of the Rhodian Corsairs, and till they were removed her naval supremacy was not complete. Genoa and Venice had

[1] See the *Story of Turkey*, 158–163.
[2] See S. LANE-POOLE, *The Art of the Saracens*, 239, &c.

been humbled : the turn of the Knights of St. John
was come. Selīm had left his son, the great Suleymān, the legacy of a splendid fleet, prepared for this
very enterprize. One hundred and three swift galleys,
thirty-five galleasses, besides smaller craft, and 107
transports, "naves, fustes, mahones, tafforées, galions,
et esquirasses," [1] formed a noble navy, and Rhodes
fell, after an heroic defence, at the close of 1522.
For six months the Knights held out, against a
fleet which had swollen to four hundred sail and an
army of over a hundred thousand men commanded
by the Sultan in person. It was a crisis in the history
of Europe : the outpost of Christendom was at bay.
The Knights realized their duty nobly, but they had
the best engineers in the world against them, and all
the resources of a now mighty empire, wielded by a
master-mind. Suleymān surrounded the city with
his works, and made regular approaches for his advancing batteries and mines ; yet at the end of a month
not a wall was down, and the eight bastions of the
eight Tongues of the Order—the English, French,
Spanish, Italian, Portuguese, German, Provençal, and
Auvergnat—were so far unmoved. Gabriel Martinego
of Candia superintended the countermines with marked
success.[2] At last the English bastion was blown up ;
the Turks swarmed to the breach, and were beaten
back with a loss of two thousand men. A second
assault failed, but on September 24th they succeeded
in getting a foothold, and the destruction of the
Spanish, Italian, and Provençal bastions by the

---

[1] *Doria et Barberousse*, Pt. II., ch. vii.
[2] *Ibid.*, Pt. II., ch. vii., p. 106 ff.

Turkish mines and the consequent exposure of the
exhausted garrison rendered the defence more and
more perilous.   The Ottoman army too was suffering
severely, from disease, as well as from the deadly
weapons of the Knights, and in the hope of sparing
his men Suleymān offered the garrison life and liberty
if they would surrender the city.   At first they proudly
rejected the offer, but within a fortnight, finding their
ammunition exhausted and their numbers sadly
thinned, on December 21st they begged the Sultan
to repeat his conditions, and, with an honourable
clemency, Suleymān let them all depart unmolested
in his own ships to such ports in Europe as seemed
best to them.[1]

The fall of Rhodes removed the last obstacle to the
complete domination of the Ottoman fleet in the
eastern basin of the Mediterranean.   Henceforward
no Christian ship was safe in those waters unless by
the pleasure of the Sultan.   The old maritime
Republics were for the time reduced to impotence, and
no power existed to challenge the Ottoman supremacy
in the Aegean, Ionian, and Adriatic Seas.

Almost at the same time the brothers Barbarossa
had effected a similar triumph in the west.   The
capture of Algiers and the firm establishment of
various strong garrisons on the Barbary coast had
given the Turkish Corsairs the command of the
western basin of the Mediterranean.   Suleymān the
Magnificent saw the necessity of combination ; he
knew that Kheyr-ed-dīn could teach the Stambol

---

[1] See the *Story of Turkey*, 170 ; and the illustrations, pp. 137, 147,
171, 175, 177.

navigators and ship-builders much that they ought to learn; his Grand Vezīr Ibrahīm strenuously urged a closer relation between the Turkish powers of the east and west; and Kheyr-ed-dīn received the Imperial command to present himself at Constantinople.

VII.

DORIA AND BARBAROSSA.

1533.

KHEYR-ED-DIN was in no hurry to visit the Sublime Porte. He had to provide for the safety and government of Algiers during his absence, when exposed to the dangers both of foreign attack and internal intrigue. He had to reckon with the galleys of the Knights of St. John, who, after wandering homeless for a longer time than was at all creditable to that Christendom which they had so heroically defended at Rhodes, had finally settled in no less convenient a spot than Malta, whence they had every opportunity of harassing the operations of the Corsairs (1530). Moreover Andrea Doria was cruising about, and he was not the sort of opponent Barbarossa cared to meet by hazard. The great Genoese admiral considered it a personal duel with Kheyr-ed-din. Each held the supreme position on his own side of the water. Both were old men and had grown old in arms. Born in 1468, of a noble Genoese family, Doria was sixty-five years of age, of which nearly fifty had been spent in warfare. He had been in the Pope's guard, and had seen service under the

Duke of Urbino and Alfonso of Naples, and when he
was over forty he had taken to the sea and found
himself suddenly High Admiral of Genoa (1513). His
appointment to the command of his country's galleys
was due to his zealous services on shore, and not to
any special experience of naval affairs ; indeed the
commander of the galleys was as much a military
as a naval officer. Doria, however, late as he
adopted his profession, possessed undoubted gifts
as a seaman, and his leadership decided which
of the rival Christian Powers should rule the
Mediterranean waves. He devoted his sword to
France in 1522, when a revolution overthrew his
party in his own republic ; and so long as he was on
the French side the command of the sea, so far as it
did not belong to the Barbary Corsairs, belonged to
France. When in 1528 he judged himself and his
country ill-used by Francis I., he carried over his own
twelve galleys to the side of Charles V. ; and then
the Imperial navies once more triumphed. Doria
was the arbiter of fortune between the contending
states. Doria was the liberator of Genoa, and, refus-
ing to be her king, remained her idol and her despot.
No name struck such terror into the hearts of the
Turks ; many a ship had fallen a prey to his devour-
ing galleys, and many a Moslem slave pulled at his
oars or languished in Genoese prisons. Officially an
admiral, he was at the same time personally a Corsair,
and used his private galleys to increase his wealth.

Kheyr-ed-dīn's fame among Christians and Turks
alike was at least as great and glorious as his rival's.
He had driven the Spaniards out of Algiers and had

inflicted incalculable injuries upon the ships and shores of the Empire. Though the two had roved the same sea for twenty years, they had never met in naval combat : perhaps each had respected the other too much to risk an encounter. Long ago, when Kheyr-ed-dīn was unknown to fame, Doria had driven him from the Goletta (1513) ; and in 1531 the Genoese admiral made a descent upon Shershēl, which Kheyr-ed-dīn had been strengthening, to the great detriment and anxiety of the opposite coast of Spain The Imperialists landed in force, surprised the fort, and liberated seven hundred Christian slaves. Then, contrary to orders and heedless of the signal gun which summoned them on board, the soldiery dispersed about the town in search of pillage, and, being taken at a disadvantage by the Turks and Moriscos of the place, were driven in confusion down to the beach, only to perceive Doria's galleys rapidly pulling away. Nine hundred were slaughtered on the seashore and six hundred made prisoners. Some say that the admiral intended to punish his men for their disobedience ; others that he sighted Kheyr-ed-dīn's fleet coming to the rescue. At all events he drew off, and the two great rivals did not meet. The Genoese picked up some Barbary vessels on his way home to console him for his failure.

In the following year he retrieved his fame by a brilliant expedition to the coasts of Greece. With thirty-five sail and forty-eight galleys he attacked Coron, by way of making a diversion while Sultan Suleymān was invading Hungary,[1] and after a heavy

---

[1] See the *Story of Turkey*, 191.

ANDREA DORIA.

bombardment succeeded in landing his men on the curtain of the fort. The Turkish garrison was spared and marched out, and Mendoza was left in command, while Doria bore up to Patras and took it, occupied the castles which guard the Gulf of Corinth, and returned in triumph to Genoa before the Turkish fleet could come up with him. This was in September, 1532. In the following spring a yet more daring feat was accomplished. Coron was running short of supplies, and a Turkish fleet blockaded the port. Nevertheless Cristofero Pallavicini carried his ship in, under cover of the castle guns, and encouraged the garrison to hold out ; and Doria, following in splendid style, fought his way in, notwithstanding that half his fleet, being sailing galleons, became becalmed in the midst of the Turkish galleys, and had to be rescued in the teeth of the enemy. Lutfi Pasha was outma-noeuvred and defeated. This revictualling of Coron, says Admiral Jurien de la Gravière, was one of the skilfullest naval operations of the sixteenth century.[1]

It was clear that, while Doria had effected almost nothing against the Barbary Corsairs, he always mastered the Turks. The Sultan was eager to discover Kheyr-ed-dīn's secret of success, and counted the days till he should arrive in the Golden Horn. The Corsair, for his part, had heard enough of Doria's recent exploits to use more than his habitual caution, and he was not disposed to cheapen his value in the Sultan's eyes by a too precipitate compliance with his Majesty's command. At last, in August, 1533, having appointed Hasan Aga, a Sardinian eunuch, in

[1] *Doria et Barberousse*, Pt. II. ch. xxv.

7

whom he greatly confided, to be viceroy during his
absence, Kheyr-ed-dīn set sail from Algiers with a
few galleys; and after doing a little business on his
own account—looting Elba and picking up some
Genoese corn-ships—pursued his way, passing Malta
at a respectful distance, and coasting the Morea, till
he dropped anchor in the Bay of Salonica.[1] By his
route, which touched Santa Maura and Navarino, he
appears to have been looking for Doria, in spite of
the smallness of his own force (which had, however,
been increased by prizes); but, fortunately, perhaps,
for the Corsair, the Genoese admiral had returned to
Sicily, and the two had missed each other on the way.

Soon the eyes of the Sultan were rejoiced with the
sight of a Barbary fleet, gaily dressed with flags and
pennons, rounding Seraglio Point, and, in perfect
order, entering the deep water of the Golden Horn;
and presently Kheyr-ed-dīn and his eighteen captains
were bowing before the Grand Signior, and reaping
the rewards due to their fame and services. It was a
strange sight that day at Eski Serai,[2] and the divan
was crowded. The tried generals and statesmen of
the greatest of Ottoman emperors assembled to gaze
upon the rough sea-dogs whose exploits were on the
lips of all Europe; and most of all they scrutinized
the vigorous well-knit yet burly figure of the old man
with the bushy eyebrows and thick beard, once a

---

[1] The Spanish historians are silent on the subject of this expedition:
or, rather, Haedo positively denies it, and says that Kheyr-ed-dīn
sent an embassy to the Sultan, but did not go in person. Hājji
Khalīfa, however, is clear and detailed in his account of the visit.

[2] For an account of Stambol and the old Seraglio see the *Story of
Turkey*, 260 ff.

bright auburn, but now hoary with years and exposure
to the freaks of fortune and rough weather. In his
full and searching eye, that could blaze with ready
and unappeasable fury, they traced the resolute mind
which was to show them the way to triumphs at
sea, comparable even to those which their victorious
Sultan had won before strong walls and on the
battle plain. The Grand Vizīr Ibrahīm recognized in
Kheyr-ed-dīn the man he needed, and the Algerine
Corsair was preferred before all the admirals of
Turkey, and appointed to reconstruct the Ottoman
navy. He spent the winter in the dockyards, where
his quick eye instantly detected the faults of the
builders. The Turks of Constantinople, he found,
knew neither how to build nor how to work their
galleys.[1] Theirs were not so swift as the Christians' ;
and instead of turning sailors themselves, and navi-
gating them properly, they used to kidnap shepherds
from Arcadia and Anatolia, who had never handled
a sail or a tiller in their lives, and entrust the
navigation of their galleys to these inexperienced
hands.[2] Kheyr-ed-dīn soon changed all this. Fortunately there were workmen and timber in
abundance, and, inspiring his men with his own
marvellous energy, he laid out sixty-one galleys
during the winter, and was able to take the sea with
a fleet of eighty-four vessels in the spring. The
period of Turkish supremacy on the sea dates from
Kheyr-ed-dīn's winter in the dockyards.

[1] See Chapter XVI., below.
[2] So says Jean Chesneau, French secretary at Constantinople in 1543.
See JURIEN DE LA GRAVIÈRE, *Les Corsaires Barbaresques*, 13.

VIII.

TUNIS TAKEN AND LOST.

1534—1535.

THE dwellers on the coasts of Italy soon discovered
the new spirit in the Turkish fleet; they had now to
dread Corsairs on both hands, east as well as west.
In the summer of 1534 Kheyr-ed-dīn led his new fleet
of eighty-four galleys forth from the Golden Horn,
to flesh their appetite on a grand quest of prey.
Entering the Straits of Messina, he surprised Reggio,
and carried off ships and slaves; stormed and burnt
the castle of S. Lucida next day, and took eight
hundred prisoners; seized eighteen galleys at Cetraro;
put Sperlonga to the sword and brand, and loaded
his ships with wives and maidens. A stealthy inland
march brought the Corsairs to Fondi, where lay
Giulia Gonzaga, the young and beautiful widow of
Vespasio Colonna, Duchess of Trajetto and Countess
of Fondi. She was sister to the "heavenly Joanna
of Aragon," on whose loveliness two hundred and
eighty Italian poets and rimesters in vain exhausted
the resources of several languages;—a loveliness
shared by the sister whose device was the "Flower of
Love" amaranth blazoned on her shield. This beauty

Kheyr-ed-dīn destined for the Sultan's harem, and so secret were the Corsairs' movements that he almost surprised the fair Giulia in her bed. She had barely time to mount a horse in her shift and fly with a single attendant,—whom she afterwards condemned to death, perhaps because the beauty revealed that night had made him overbold.[1] Enraged at her escape the pirates made short work of Fondi ; the church was wrecked, and the plundering went on for four terrible hours, never to be forgotten by the inhabitants.

Refreshed and excited by their successful raid, the Turks needed little encouragement to enter with heartiness upon the real object of the expedition, which was nothing less than the annexation of the kingdom of Tunis. Three centuries had passed since the Sultans of the race of Hafs had established their authority on the old Carthaginian site, upon the breaking up of the African empire of the Almohades. Their rule had been mild and just ; they had main-tained on the whole friendly relations with the European powers, and many treaties record the fair terms upon which the merchants of Pisa, Venice, and Genoa were admitted to the port of Tunis. Saint Louis had been so struck with the piety and justice of the king that he had even come to convert him, and had died in the attempt. Twenty-one rulers of their line had succeeded one another, till the vigour of the Benī-Hafs was sapped, and fraternal jealousies added bloodshed to weakness. Hasan, the twenty-second, stepped to the throne over the bodies of forty-four slaughtered brothers, and when

[1] Von Hammer, *Gesch. d. Osm. Reiches*, ii. 129.

he had thus secured his place he set a pattern of
vicious feebleness for all sovereigns to avoid. A rival
claimant served as the Corsair's pretext for invasion,
and Kheyr-ed-dīn had hardly landed when this
miserable wretch fled the city, and though supported
by some of the Arab tribes he could make no head
against the Turkish guns. Tunis, like Algiers, had
been added to the Ottoman Empire, against its will,
and by the same masterful hands. It may be doubted
whether the Sultan's writ would have run in either of
his new provinces had their conqueror gainsaid it.

Tunis did not long remain in the possession of
Barbarossa. The banished king appealed to Charles
V., and, whatever the emperor may have thought of
Hasan's wrongs, he plainly perceived that Barbarossa's presence in Tunis harbour was a standing
menace to his own kingdom of Sicily. It was bad
enough to see nests of pirates perched upon the rocks
of the Algerine coast ; but Tunis was the key of the
passage from the west to the eastern basin of the
Mediterranean, and to leave it in the Corsairs' hands
was to the last degree hazardous. Accordingly he
espoused the cause of Hasan, and at the end of May,
1535, he set sail from Barcelona with six hundred
ships commanded by Doria (who had his own grudge
to settle), and carrying the flower of the Imperial
troops, Spaniards, Italians, and Germans. In June
he laid siege to the Goletta—or *halk-el-wēd,* "throat
of the torrent," as the Arabs called it—those twin
towers a mile asunder which guarded the channel of
Tunis. The great carack *St. Ann,* sent, with four
galleys, by " the Religion " (so the Knights of Malta

TUNIS, 1566.

(*From a Map in the British Museum.*)

styled their Order), was moored close in, and her
heavy cannon soon made a breach, through which
the Chevalier Cossier led the Knights of St. John,
who always claimed the post of danger, into the
fortress, and planted the banner of "the Religion"
on the battlements [1] (14 July). Three desperate
sallies had the besieged made under the leadership of
Sinān the Jew ; three Italian generals of rank had
fallen in the melley ; before they were driven in
confusion back upon the city of Tunis, leaving the
Goletta with all its stores of weapons and ammunition,
and its forty guns, some of them famous for their
practice at the siege of Rhodes, and more than a
hundred vessels, in the hands of the enemy. Barbarossa came out to meet the emperor at the head of
nearly ten thousand troops ; but his Berbers refused
to fight, the thousands of Christian slaves in the
Kasaba (or citadel), aided by treachery, broke their
chains and shut the gates behind him ; and, after
defending his rampart as long as he could, the
Corsair chief, with Sinān and Aydīn "Drub-Devil,"
made his way to Bona, where he had fortunately left
fifteen of his ships. The lines of Kheyr-ed-dīn's
triple wall may still be traced across the neck of land
which separates the lake of Tunis from the Mediterranean. Fifteen years ago this rampart was cut
through, when nearly two hundred skeletons, some
Spanish money, cannon balls, and broken weapons
were found outside it.[2]

[1] BROADLEY, *Tunis, Past and Present*, i. 42, quoting a narrative by
Boyssat, one of the Knights of Malta, written in 1612.

[2] On Charles's expedition to Tunis, consult Marmol, Hājji Khalifa,
Robertson, Morgan, Von Hammer, and Broadley. In the last

For three days Charles gave up the city of Tunis
to the brutality of his soldiers. They were days of
horrible license and bloodshed. Men, women, and
children were massacred, and worse than massacred,
in thousands. The infuriated troops fought one with
the other for the possession of the spoil, and the
luckless Christians of the Kasaba were cut down by
their deliverers in the struggle for Kheyr-ed-dīn's
treasures. The streets became shambles, the houses
dens of murder and shame : the very Catholic
chroniclers admit the abominable outrages committed
by the licentious and furious soldiery of the great
Emperor. It is hard to remember that almost at
the very time when German and Spanish and Italian
men-at-arms were outraging and slaughtering helpless, innocent people in Tunis, who had taken little or
no hand in Kheyr-ed-dīn's wars and had accepted his
authority with reluctance, the Grand Vezīr Ibrahīm
was entering Baghdād and Tebrīz as a conqueror at
the head of wild Asiatic troops, and not a house nor
a human being was molested. *Fas est et ab hoste
doceri.*

So far as Tunis was concerned the expedition of
Charles V. was fruitless. Before he sailed in August
he made a treaty with Hasan, which stipulated for
tribute to Spain, the possession of the Goletta by the
crown of Castile, the freeing of Christian slaves, the
cessation of piracy, and the payment of homage by

will be found some interesting photographs of Jan Cornelis Ver-
meyen's pictures, painted on the spot during the progress of the siege,
by command of the Emperor, and now preserved at Windsor. All the
accounts of the siege and capture show discrepancies which it seems
hopeless to reconcile.

an annual tribute of six Moorish barbs and twelve
falcons ; and he and the Moor duly swore it on Cross
and sword. But the treaty was so much parchment
wasted. No Moslem prince who had procured his
restoration by such means as Hasan had used, who
had spilt Moslem blood with Christian weapons and
ruined Moslem homes by the sacrilegious atrocities
of "infidel" soldiers, and had bound himself the
vassal of "idolatrous" Spain, could hope to keep his
throne long. He was an object of horror and
repulsion to the people upon whom he had brought
this awful calamity, and so fierce was their scorn of
the traitor to Islam that the story is told of a
Moorish girl in the clutch of the soldiers, who, when
the restored King of Tunis sought to save her, spat in
his face ; anything was better than the dishonour of
his protection. Hasan pretended to reign for five
years, but the country was in arms, holy Kayrawān
would have nothing to say to a governor who owed
his throne to infidel ravishers ; Imperial troops in
vain sought to keep him there ; Doria himself succeeded only for a brief while in reducing the coast
towns to the wretched prince's authority; and in 1540
Hasan was imprisoned and blinded by his son
Hamīd, and none can pity him. The coast was in
the possession of the Corsairs, and, as we shall see,
even the Spaniards were forced ere long to abandon
the Goletta.

Nevertheless, the expedition to Tunis was a feat of
which Europe was proud. Charles V. seldom suffered
from depreciation of his exploits, and, as Morgan
quaintly says, " I have never met with that Spaniard

in my whole life, who, I am persuaded, would not
have bestowed on me at least forty *Boto a Christo's,*
had I pretended to assert Charles V. not to have held
this whole universal globe in a string for four-and-
twenty hours ; and *then it broke :* though none had
ever the good nature or manners to inform or correct
my ignorance in genuine history, by letting me into
the secret when that critical and slippery period of
time was." [1]　　Naturally admirers so thoroughgoing
made the most of the conquest of Tunis, the
reduction of the formidable Goletta, the release of
thousands of Christian captives, and, above all, the
discomfiture of that scourge of Christendom, Barbarossa himself.　Poets sang of it, a painter-in-
ordinary depicted the siege, a potter at Urbino burnt
the scene into his vase ; all Europe was agog with
enthusiasm at the feat.　Charles posed as a
crusader and a knight-errant, and commemorated
his gallant deeds and those of his gentlemen by
creating a new order of chivalry, the Cross of Tunis,
with the motto " Barbaria," of which however we
hear no more.　Altogether " it was a famous victory."

The joy of triumph was sadly marred by the
doings of Kheyr-ed-dīn.　That incorrigible pirate,
aware that no one would suspect that he could
be roving while Charles was besieging his new
kingdom, took occasion to slip over to Minorca
with his twenty-seven remaining galleots ; and there,
flying Spanish and other false colours, deceived the
islanders into the belief that his vessels were part
of the Armada ; upon which he rowed boldly into

[1] *Hist. of Algiers,* 286.

Port Mahon, seized a rich Portuguese galleon, sacked the town, and, laden with six thousand captives and much booty and ammunition, led his prize back in triumph to Algiers. In the meanwhile Doria was assiduously hunting for him with thirty galleys, under the emperor's express orders to catch him dead or alive. The great Genoese had to wait yet three years for his long-sought duel.

Having accomplished its object, the Armada, as usual, broke up without making a decisive end of the Corsairs. Kheyr-ed-dîn, waiting at Algiers in expectation of attack, heard the news gladly, and, when the coast was clear, sailed back to Constantinople for reinforcements. He never saw Algiers again.

IX.

THE SEA-FIGHT OFF PREVESA.

1537.

WHEN Barbarossa returned to Constantinople
Tunis was forgotten and Minorca alone called to
mind: instead of the title of Beglerbeg of Algiers,
the Sultan saluted him as Capudan Pasha or High
Admiral of the Ottoman fleets. There was work to
be done in the Adriatic, and none was fitter to do it
than the great Corsair. Kheyr-ed-dīn had acquired
an added influence at Stambol since the execution of
the Grand Vezīr Ibrahīm,[1] and he used it in exactly
the opposite direction. Ibrahīm, a Dalmatian by
birth, had always striven to maintain frie dly
relations with Venice, his native state, and for more
than thirty years there had been peace between the
Republic and the Porte. Barbarossa, on the contrary,
longed to pit his galleys against the most famous of
the maritime nations of the Middle Ages, and to
make the Crescent as supreme in the waters of the
Adriatic as it was in the Aegean. Francis I. was
careful to support this policy out of his jealousy of

---

[1] See the *Story of Turkey*, 195.

the Empire. The Venetians, anxious to keep on good terms with the Sultan, and to hold a neutral position between Francis and Charles V., found themselves gradually committed to a war, and by their own fault. Their commanders in the Adriatic and at Candia were unable to resist the temptation of chasing Ottoman merchantmen. Canale, the Proveditore of Candia, caught a noted Corsair, the " Young Moor of Alexander," as his victims called him, sunk or captured his galleys, killed his Janis-saries, and severely wounded the young Moor him-self ;—and all this in Turkish waters, on Turkish subjects, and in time of peace. Of course when the too gallant Proveditore came to his senses and per-ceived his folly, he patched the young Moor's wounds and sent him tenderly back to Algiers : but the Sultan's ire was already roused, and when Venetian galleys actually gave chase to a ship that carried a Turkish ambassador, no apologies that the Signoria offered could wipe out the affront. War was in-evitable, and Venice hastily made common cause with the Pope and the Emperor against the formid-able host which now advanced upon the Adriatic.

Before this, some stirring actions had been fought off the coasts of Greece. Doria, sallying forth from Messina, had met the governor of Gallipoli off Paxos, and had fought him before daybreak. Standing erect on the poop, conspicuous in his cramoisy doublet, the tall figure of the old admiral was seen for an hour and a half directing the conflict, sword in hand, an easy mark for sharpshooters, as a wound in the knee reminded him. After a severe struggle the

twelve galleys of the enemy were captured and
carried in triumph to Messina. Barbarossa was
sorely wanted now, and in May, 1537, he sailed with
one hundred and thirty-five galleys to avenge the
insult. For a whole month he laid waste the Apulian
coast like a pestilence, and carried off ten thousand
slaves, while Doria lay helpless with a far inferior
force in Messina roads. The Turks were boasting
that they might soon set up a Pope of their own,
when the war with Venice broke out, and they were
called off from their devastation of Italy by the
Sultan's command to besiege Corfu. The Ionian
islands were always a bone of contention between the
Turks and their neighbours, and a war with Venice
naturally began with an attack upon Corfu. The
Senate had shut its eyes as long as possible to the
destination of the huge armaments which had left
Constantinople in the spring : Tunis, or perhaps
Naples, was said to be their object. But now they
were undeceived, and on the 25th of August, Captain
Pasha Barbarossa landed twenty-five thousand men
and thirty cannon under Lutfi Pasha, three miles
from the castle of Corfu. Four days later the Grand
Vezīr Ayās, with twenty-five thousand more and a
brilliant staff, joined the first-comers, and the Akinji
or light troops spread fire and sword around. A
fifty-pounder fired nineteen shots in three days, but
only five struck the fortress: the Turks fired too high,
and many of their missiles fell harmlessly into the
sea beyond. In spite of storm and rain the Grand
Vezīr would not desist from making the round of the
trenches by night. Suleymān offered liberal terms

of capitulation, but the besieged sent back his messenger with never an answer. Alexandro Tron worked the big guns of the castle with terrible precision. Two galleys were quickly sunk, four men were killed in the trenches by a single shot—a new and alarming experience in those early days of gunnery—four times the Fort of St. Angelo was attacked in vain ; winter was approaching, and the Sultan determined to raise the siege. In vain Barbarossa remonstrated : "A thousand such castles were not worth the life of one of his brave men," said the Sultan, and on the 17th of September the troops began to re-embark.[1]

Then began a scene of devastation such as the isles of Greece have too often witnessed,—not from Turks only, but from Genoese and Venetians, who also came to the Archipelago for their oarsmen,—but never perhaps on so vast a scale. Butrinto was burnt, Paxos conquered, and then Barbarossa carried fire and sword throughout the Adriatic and the Archipelago. With seventy galleys and thirty galleots, he raged among the islands, most of which belonged to noble families of Venice—the Venieri, Grispi, Pisani, Quirini. Syra, Skyros, Aegina, Paros, Naxos, Tenos, and other Venetian possessions were overwhelmed, and thousands of their people carried off to pull a Turkish oar. Naxos contributed five thousand dollars as her first year's tribute ; Aegina furnished six thousand slaves. Many trophies did Barbarossa bring home to Stambol, whose riches certainly did his own and the Sultan's, if not "the general coffer, fill."

[1] Von Hammer, *Gesch. d. Osm. Reiches*, ii. 142.

Four hundred thousand pieces of gold, a thousand girls, and fifteen hundred boys, were useful resources when he returned to " rub his countenance against the royal stirrup." [1] Two hundred boys in scarlet, bearing gold and silver bowls; thirty more laden with purses ; two hundred with rolls of fine cloth : such was the present with which the High Admiral approached the Sultan's presence.

Suleymān's genius was at that time bent upon three distinct efforts : he was carrying on a compaign in Moldavia ; his Suez fleet—a novelty in Ottoman history—was invading the Indian Ocean, with no very tangible result, it is true (unless a trophy of Indian ears and noses may count), save the conquest of Aden on the return voyage, but still a notable exploit, and disturbing to the Portuguese in Gujerat ; and his High Admiral was planning the destruction of the maritime power of Venice.

In the summer of 1538, Barbarossa put off to sea, and soon had one hundred and fifty sail under his command. He began by collecting rowers and tribute from the islands, twenty-five of which had now been transferred from the Venetian to the Turkish allegiance, and then laid waste eighty villages in Candia. Here news was brought that the united fleet of the Emperor, Venice, and the Pope was, cruising in the Adriatic, and the Captain Pasha hastened to meet it. The pick of the Corsairs was with him. Round his flagship were ranged the galleys of Dragut, Murād Reïs, Sinān, Sālih Reïs with twenty Egyptian vessels, and others, to the number of one hundred

[1] Hāɪjı Khalīfa, 58.

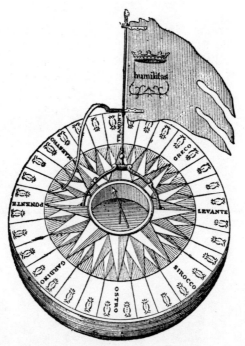

COMPASS OF THE SIXTEENTH CENTURY.
(*Jurien de la Gravière.*)

and twenty-two ships of war. The advance guard sighted part of the enemy off Prevesa—a Turkish fortress opposite the promontory of Arta or Actium, where Antony suffered his memorable defeat.

The Christian strength was really overwhelming. Eighty Venetian, thirty-six Papal, and thirty Spanish galleys, together with fifty sailing galleons, made up a formidable total of nearly two hundred ships of war, and they carried scarcely less than sixty thousand men, and two thousand five hundred guns. Doria was in chief command, and Capello and Grimani led the Venetian and Roman contingents. Barbarossa had fortunately received but an imperfect report of the enemy's strength and so boldly pursued his northerly course up the Adriatic. When he reached Prevesa, the combined fleets had gone on to Corfu, and he was able to enter unopposed the spacious gulf of Arta, where all the navies of the world might safely anchor and defy pursuit.

On September 25th, the allied fleets appeared off the entrance to the gulf, and then for the first time Barbarossa realized his immense good fortune in being the first in the bay. Outnumbered as he was, a fight in the open sea might have ended in the total destruction of his navy ; but secure in an ample harbour, on a friendly coast, behind a bar which the heavier vessels of the enemy could not cross, he could wait his opportunity and take the foe at a disadvantage. The danger was that Doria might disembark his guns and attack from the shores of the gulf, and to meet this risk some of the Turkish captains insisted on landing their men and trying

to erect earthworks for their protection; but the
fire from the Christian ships soon stopped this
manoeuvre. Barbarossa had never expected Doria
to hazard a landing, and he was right. The old
admiral of Charles V. was not likely to expose his
ships to the risk of a sally from the Turks just when
he had deprived them of the men and guns that could
alone defend them.

The two fleets watched each other warily. Doria
and Barbarossa had at last come face to face for
a great battle, but, strange as it may seem, neither
cared to begin : Barbarossa was conscious of serious
numerical inferiority; Doria was anxious for the
safety of his fifty big sailing vessels, on the heavy
artillery of which he most relied, but which a contrary
wind might drive to destruction on the hostile coast.
As it was, his guideship on the extreme left had but
a fathom of water under her keel. Each felt keenly
the weighty responsibility of his position, and even
the sense that now at last the decisive day of their
long rivalry had come could not stir them from their
policy of prudence. Moreover, it was no longer a
question of the prowess of hot-blooded youth : Doria
and Barbarossa and Capello were all men of nearly
seventy years, and Doria was certainly not the man
he once was ; politics had spoilt him.

So the two great admirals waited and eyed each
other's strength. Will Barbarossa come out ? Or must
Doria risk the passage of the bar and force his way in
to the encounter ? Neither event happened : but on the
morning of the 27th the Corsairs rubbed their eyes
to feel if they were asleep, as they saw the whole

magnificent navy of Christendom, anchor a-peak, sailing slowly and majestically—*away!* Were the Christians afraid? Anyhow no one, not even Barbarossa, could hold the Turks back now. Out they rushed in hot pursuit, not thinking or caring—save their shrewd captain—whether this were not a feint of Doria's to catch them in the open. "Get into line," said Barbarossa to his captains, "and do as you see me do." Dragut took the right wing, Sālih Reïs the left. Early on the 28th the Christian fleet was discovered at anchor, in a foul wind, off Santa Maura, thirty miles to the south. Doria was not at all prepared for such prompt pursuit, and eyed with anxiety the long battle line of one hundred and forty galleys, galleots, and brigantines, bearing down upon him before the wind. His ships were scattered, for the sails could not keep up with the oars, and Condulmiero's huge Venetian carack was becalmed off Zuara, a long way behind, and others were in no better plight. Three hours Doria hesitated, and then gave the order to sail north and meet the enemy. Condulmiero was already fiercely engaged, and soon his carack was a mere unrigged helmless waterlog, only saved from instant destruction by her immense size and terrific guns, which, well aimed, low on the water, to gain the *ricochet*, did fearful mischief among the attacking galleys. Two galleons were burnt to the water's edge, and their crews took to the boats; a third, Boccanegra's, lost her mainmast, and staggered away crippled. What was Doria about? The wind was now in his favour; the enemy was in front: but Doria continued to tack and manoeuvre at

a distance.   What he aimed at is uncertain : his colleagues Grimani and Capello went on board his flagship, and vehemently remonstrated with him, and
even implored him to depart and let them fight the
battle with their own ships, but in vain.   He was
bent on tactics, when what was needed was pluck ;
and tactics lost the day.   The Corsairs took, it is
true, only seven galleys and sail-
ing vessels, but they held the sea.
Doria sailed away in the evening
for Corfu, and the whole allied
fleet followed in a gale of wind.[1]

So, after all, the great duel was
never fairly fought between the
sea-rivals.   Barbarossa was willing, but Doria held back : he
preferred to show his seamanship instead of his courage.   The
result was in effect a victory, a
signal victory, for the Turks.
Two hundred splendid vessels

OBSERVATION WITH
THE ASTROLABE.
(*Jurien de la Gravière.*)

of three great Christian states had fled before an
inferior force of Ottomans; and it is no wonder
that Sultan Suleymān, when he learnt the news at
Yamboli, illuminated the town, and added one hundred thousand aspres a year to the revenues of the
conqueror.   Barbarossa had once more proved to
the world that the Turkish fleet was invincible.
The flag of Suleymān floated supreme in all the
waters of the Mediterranean Sea.

[1] JURIEN DE LA GRAVIÈRE, *Doria et Barberousse*, Pt. II., ch.
xlii.-xlv. ; HĀJJI KHALIFA, 62 ; VON HAMMER, ii. 155 ; MORGAN, 290.

X.

BARBAROSSA IN FRANCE.

1539—1546.

BARBAROSSA'S life was drawing to a close, but in the eight years that remained he enhanced his already unrivalled renown. His first exploit after Prevesa was the recapture of Castelnuovo, which the allied fleets had seized in October, as some compensation on land for their humiliation at sea. The Turkish armies had failed to recover the fortress in January, 1539; but in July Barbarossa went to the front as usual, with a fleet of two hundred galleys, large and small, and all his best captains; and, after some very pretty fighting in the Gulf of Cattaro, landed eighty-four of his heaviest guns and bombarded Castelnuovo, from three well-placed batteries. On August 7th, a sanguinary assault secured the first line of the defences; three days later the governor, Don Francisco Sarmiento, and his handful of Spaniards, surrendered to a final assault, and were surprised to find themselves chivalrously respected as honourable foes. Three thousand Spaniards had fallen, and eight thousand Turks, in the course of the siege.

One more campaign and Barbarossa's feats are over. Great events were happening on the Algerine coasts, where we must return after too long an absence in the Levant and Adriatic: but first the order of years must be neglected that we may see the last of the most famous of all the Corsairs. To make amends for the coldness of Henry VIII., Francis I. was allied with the other great maritime power, Turkey, against the Emperor, in 1543; and the old sea rover actually brought his fleet of one hundred and fifty ships to Marseilles. The French captains saluted the Corsair's *capitana*, and the banner of Our Lady was lowered to be replaced by the Crescent. Well may a French admiral call this "the impious alliance." On his way Barbarossa enjoyed a raid in quite his old style; burnt Reggio and carried off the governor's daughter; appeared off the Tiber, and terrified the people of Cività Vecchia; and in July entered the Gulf of Lyons in triumph. Here he found the young Duke of Enghien, François de Bourbon, commander of the French galleys, who received him with all honour and ceremony.

Barbarossa had hardly arrived when he discovered that his great expedition was but a fool's errand. The King of France was afraid of attempting a serious campaign against the Emperor, and he was already ashamed of his alliance with the Musulmans: his own subjects—nay, all Europe—were crying shame. Barbarossa grew crimson with fury, and tore his white beard: he had not come with a vast fleet all the way from Stambol to be made a laughing-

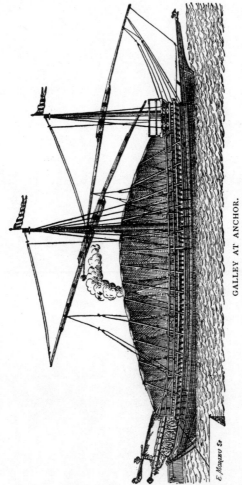

GALLEY AT ANCHOR.
(*Jurien de la Gravière.*)

E. Morin Sr

stock. Something must evidentially be done to satisfy his honour, and Francis I. unwillingly gave orders for the bombardment of Nice. Accompanied by a feeble and ill-prepared French contingent, which soon ran short of ammunition—"Fine soldiers," cried the Corsair, "to fill their ships with wine casks, and leave the powder barrels behind!"—Barbarossa descended upon the Gate of Italy. The city soon surrendered, but the fort held out, defended by one of those invincible foes of the Turk, a Knight of Malta, Paolo Simeoni, who had himself experienced captivity at the hands of Barbarossa ; and as the French protested against sacking the town after capitulating on terms, and as Charles's relieving army was advancing, the camps were broken up in confusion, and the fleets retired from Nice.

The people of Toulon beheld a strange spectacle that winter. The beautiful harbour of Provence was allotted to the Turkish admiral for his winter quarters. There, at anchor, lay the immense fleet of the Grand Signior ; and who knew how long it might dominate the fairest province of France? There, turbaned Musulmans paced the decks and bridge, below and beside which hundreds of Christian slaves sat chained to the bench and victims to the lash of the boatswain. Frenchmen were forced to look on, helplessly, while Frenchmen groaned in the infidels' galleys, within the security of a French port. The captives died by hundreds of fever during that winter, but no Christian burial was allowed them—even the bells that summon the pious to the Mass were silenced, for are they not "the devil's

musical instrument " ? [1]—and the gaps in the benches
were filled by nightly raids among the neighbouring
villages. It was ill sleeping around Toulon when
the Corsair press-gangs were abroad. And to feed
and pay these rapacious allies was a task that went
near to ruining the finances of France.

The French were not satisfied of the Corsair's
fidelity, and it must be added that the Emperor
might have had some reason to doubt the honesty
of Doria. The two greatest admirals of the age
were both in the Western Mediterranean, but nothing
could tempt them to come to blows. The truth
was that each had a great reputation to lose, and
each preferred to go to his grave with all his fame
undimmed. Francis I. had a suspicion that Barbarossa was meditating the surrender of Toulon to the
Emperor, and, improbable as it was, some colour
was given to the King's anxiety by the amicable
relations which seemed to subsist between the
Genoese Corsair and his Barbary rival. Doria gave
up the captive Dragut to his old captain for a
ransom of three thousand gold crowns—a transaction
on which he afterwards looked back with unqualified
regret. The situation was growing daily more un-
pleasant for France. From his easy position in
Toulon, Barbarossa sent forth squadrons under Sālih
Reïs and other commanders to lay waste the coasts
of Spain, while he remained "lazily engaged in
emptying the coffers of the French king."

At last they got rid of him. Francis was com-

[1] See S. LANE-POOLE, *The Speeches and Tabletalk of the Prophet
Mohammad*, 168.

pelled to furnish the pay and rations of the whole crews and troops of the Ottoman fleet up to their re-entry into the Bosphorus ; he had to free four hundred Mohammedan galley slaves and deliver them to Barbarossa ; he loaded him with jewellery, silks, and other presents ; the Corsair departed in a Corsair's style, weighed down with spoil. His homeward voyage was one long harrying of the Italian coasts ; his galley sailed low with human freight ; and his arrival at Constantinople was the signal for the filling of all the harems of the great pashas with beautiful captives. Barbarossa, laden with such gifts, was sure of his welcome.

Two years later he died, in July, 1546, an old man of perhaps near ninety, yet without surviving his great fame. "Valorous yet prudent, furious in attack, foreseeing in preparation," he ranks as the first sea captain of his time. "The chief of the sea is dead," expressed in three Arabic words, gives the numerical value 953, the year of the Hijra in which Kheyr-ed-dīn Barbarossa died.

Long afterwards no Turkish fleet left the Golden Horn without her crew repeating a prayer and firing a salute over the tomb at Beshiktash, where lie the bones of the first great Turkish admiral.

XI.

CHARLES AT ALGIERS.

1541.

WHEN Barbarossa left Algiers for ever in 1535 to become the High Admiral of the Ottoman Empire, the Corsairs lost indeed their chief; but so many of his captains remained behind that the game of sea roving went on as merrily as ever. Indeed so fierce and ruthless were their depredations that the people of Italy and Spain and the islands began to regret the attentions of so gentlemanly a robber as Barbarossa. His successor or viceroy at Algiers was a Sardinian renegade, Hasan the Eunuch; but the chief commanders at sea were Dragut, Sālih Reïs, Sinān, and the rest, who, when not called to join the Captain Pasha's fleet, pursued the art of piracy from the Barbary coast. Dragut (properly Torghūd) worked measureless mischief in the Archipelago and Adriatic, seized Venetian galleys and laid waste the shores of Italy, till he was caught by Giannettino Doria, nephew of the great admiral, while unsuspectingly engaged in dividing his spoils on the Sardinian coast (1540). Incensed to find his vast empire perpetually harassed by foes so lawless and in numbers so puny, Charles the Emperor resolved to put down the Corsairs' trade once and for ever. He had subdued Tunis in 1535, but piracy still went on. Now he would grapple the head and front of the offence, and conquer Algiers.

He had no fears of the result; the Corsair city would fall at the mere sight of his immense flotilla; and in this vainglorious assurance he set out in October, 1541. He even took Spanish ladies on board to view his triumph. The season for a descent on the African coast was over, and every one knew that the chance of effecting anything before the winter storms should guard the coast from any floating enemy was more than doubtful; but "the Spaniards commonly move with gravity"; and besides, Charles had been delayed during a busy summer by his troubles in Germany and Flanders, and could not get away before.

Now at last he was free; and, in spite of the earnest remonstrances of Doria and the entreaties of the Pope, to Algiers he would go. Everything had long been prepared—a month, he believed, at the outside would finish the matter—in short, go he would. At Spezzia he embarked on Doria's flag-ship; the Duke of Alva, of sanguinary memory, commanded the troops, many of whom had been brought by the Emperor himself from the German highlands. Ill-luck attended them from the outset: a storm, no unusual phenomenon with November coming on, drove the ships back into shelter at Corsica. At length the seas subsided, and the fleet, picking up allies as it went along, cautiously hugged the land as far as Minorca, where the mistral, the terror of seamen, rushed down upon the huge armada—masts strained, yards cracked, sails were torn to rags, and there was nothing for it but to row —row for their lives and for Charles. They were but seven miles from Port Mahon, yet it took half the night to win there—an endless night which the panting crews never forgot.

In the bay of Palma, at Majorca, the fleet was assembled. There were the Emperor's hundred sailing vessels carrying the German and Italian troops, commanded by such historic names as Colonna and Spinosa ; there were Fernando Gonzago's Sicilian galleys, and a hundred and fifty transports from Naples and Palermo ; there were the fifty galleys of Bernadino de Mendoza, conveying two hundred transports with the arms and artillery, and carrying the corps of gentlemen adventurers, mustered from the chivalry of Spain, and including one only who had climbed up from the ranks—but that one was Cortes, the conqueror of Mexico. Over five hundred sail, manned by twelve thousand men, and carrying a land force of twenty-four thousand soldiers, entered the roads of Algiers on October 19, 1541.

At last the great Emperor set eyes upon the metropolis of piracy. On the rocky promontory which forms the western crest of the crescent bay, high up the amphitheatre of hills, tier upon tier, in their narrow overshadowed lanes, the houses of the Corsairs basked in the autumn sun, crowned by the

SIEGE OF ALGIERS, 1541.

(*From a map in the British Museum.*)

fortress which had known the imperious rule of two
Barbarossas. On the right was the mole which
Spanish slaves had built out of the ruins of the
Spanish fort. Two gates fronted the south and
north, the Bab Azūn and Bab el-Wēd.

Avoiding the promontory of Cashina, the galleys,
with furled sails, drew up before the low strand,
backed by stretches of luxuriant verdure, south of
the city, and out of range, at the spot which is still
called the "Jardin d'essai." A heavy swell prevented their landing for three days, but on the 23rd,
in beautiful weather, the troops disembarked. The
Berbers and Arabs, who had lined the shore and
defied the invaders, hastily retired before the guns of
the galleys, and the Spaniards landed unopposed.
The next day they began the march to the city some
few miles off. The Spaniards formed the left wing
on the hill side ; the Emperor and the Duke of Alva
with the German troops composed the centre ; the
Italians and one hundred and fifty knights of Malta
marched on the right by the seashore. Driving
back the straggling bands of mounted Arabs, who
ambushed among the rocks and ravines, and picked
off many of the Christians, the invaders pushed
steadily on, till Algiers was invested on all sides
save the north. Its fate appeared sealed. A brief
bombardment from Charles's heavy cannon, and the
Spaniards would rush the breach and storm the
citadel. Hasan Aga, within, with only eight
hundred Turks, and perhaps five thousand Arabs and
Moors, must almost have regretted the proud reply he
had just made to the Emperor's summons to surrender.

Then, when the end seemed close at hand, the forces of Nature came to the rescue. The stars in their courses fought for Algiers : the rains descended and the winds blew and beat upon that army, till the wretched soldiers, with neither tents nor cloaks, with barely food—for the landing of the stores had hardly begun—standing all night knee-deep in slush in that pinguid soil, soaked to the skin, frozen by the driving rain and bitter wind, were ready to drop with exhaustion and misery. When morning dawned they could scarcely bear up against the blustering gale ; their powder was wet ; and a sudden sally of the Turks spread a panic in the sodden ranks which needed all the courage and coolness of the Knights of Malta to compose. At last the enemy was driven out of the trenches and pursued, skirmishing all the way, to the Bab Azūn. It looked as though pursuers and pursued would enter together ; but the gate was instantly shut, and a daring Knight of Malta had barely struck his dagger in the gate to defy the garrison, when the Christians found themselves under so heavy a fire from the battlements, that they were forced to beat a retreat : the Knights of Malta, last of all, their scarlet doublets shining like a fresh wound, and their faces to the foe, covered the retreat.

Hasan then led out his best horsemen from the gate, and driving their heels into their horses' flanks, the cloud of Moslems poured down the hill. The Knights of Malta bore the shock with their iron firmness, though they lost heavily. The Italians ran for their lives. The Germans whom Charles hurriedly despatched to the rescue came back at the double without drawing a sword. The Emperor himself put on his armour, spurred his charger into the midst of the fugitives, sword in hand, and with vehement reproaches succeeded in shaming them into fight. " Come, gentlemen," then said he to the nobles around, " forwards !" And thus he led his dispirited troops once more to the field ; this time the panic alarm of the rank and file was controlled and banished by the cool courage of the cavaliers, and the Turks were driven back into the town. The skirmish had cost him three hundred men and a dozen Knights of Malta. All that day the Emperor and his officers, great signiors all, stood at arms in the pouring rain, with the water oozing from their boots, vigilantly alert.

Had Charles now run his ships ashore at all hazard, and dragged up his heavy siege train and stores and tents and ammunition, all might yet have been won. But several precious days were wasted, and on the morning of the 25th such a storm sprang up as mortal mariner rarely encountered even off such a coast—a violent north-easterly hurricane—still known in Algiers as " Charles's gale "—such as few vessels cared to ride off a lee shore. The immense flotilla in the bay was within an ace of total destruction. Anchors and cables were powerless to hold the crowded, jostling ships. One after the other they broke loose, and keeled over to the tempest till their decks were drowned in the seas. Planks gaped ; broadside to broadside the helpless hulks crashed together. Many of the crews threw themselves madly on shore. In six hours one hundred and fifty ships sank. The rowers of the

galleys, worn out with toiling at the oar, at last succumbed, and fifteen of the vessels ran on shore,
only to be received by the Berbers of the hills, who
ran their spears through the miserable shipwrecked
sailors as soon as they gained the land.

The worst day must come to an end: on the
morrow the storm was over, and Doria, who had
succeeded in taking the greater part of the fleet out
to sea, came back to see what new folly was in hand.
He was indignant with the Emperor for having
rejected his advice and so led the fleet and army into
such peril; he was disgusted with his captains, who
had completely lost their coolness in the hurricane,
and wanted to run their vessels ashore, with the
certainty of wreck, sooner than ride out the storm—
and yet called themselves sailors!

He found Charles fully aware of the necessity for a
temporary retreat, till the army should be revictualled
and reclothed. The camp was struck: the Emperor
himself watched the operation, standing at the door
of his tent in a long white cassock, murmuring quietly
the Christian's consolation: "Thy will be done"—
Fiat voluntas Tua! Baggage and ordnance were
abandoned; the horses of the field artillery were
devoured by the hungry troops; and then the march
began.

To retreat at all is humiliation, but to retreat as
this luckless army did was agony. Deep mud clogged
their weary feet; when a halt was called they could
but rest on their halberts, to lie down was to be
suffocated in filth; mountain torrents swollen breast-
high had to be crossed, the wading men were washed

away till they built a rude bridge—O crowning humiliation!—out of the wreckage of their own ships. Hasan and a multitude of Turks and Arabs hung forever on their flanks. The dejected Italians, who had no stomach for this sort of work, fell often into the hands of the pursuers; the Germans, who could do nothing without their customary internal stuffing, were mere *impedimenta;* and only the lean Spaniard covered the retreat with something of his natural courage.

At last the dejected army reached the Bay of Temendefust (Matifoux), where the remains of the fleet were lying at anchor. It was resolved, in view of the approach of winter and the impossibility of sending supplies to an army in stormy weather, to reëmbark. Cortes in vain protested : the council of war agreed that it was too late in the year to attempt retaliation. Then a new difficulty arose : how was room to be found in a flotilla, which had lost nearly a third of its ships, for an army which was but a couple of thousand less than when it landed ? Regretfully Charles gave orders for the horses to be cast into the sea, and, despite their masters' entreaties, favourite chargers of priceless value were slaughtered and thrown overboard. The famous breed of Spanish horses was well-nigh ruined. It was but one tragedy more. On the 2nd of November most of the troops were on board. Charles resolved to be the last to leave the strand ; but the wind was getting up, the sea rising, and at last he gave the order to weigh anchor. Often is the story told in Algiers how the great Emperor, who would fain hold Europe in the palm

of his hand, sadly took the crown from off his head
and casting it into the sea said, "Go, bauble : let
some more fortunate prin :e redeem and wear thee."

He did not sail a moment too soon. A new and
terrific storm burst forth. The ships were driven
hither and thither. Where the tempest drove them,
there they helplessly wandered, and many men died
from famine and exposure. Some of the Spanish
vessels were wrecked at Algiers, and their crews and
troops were sent to the bagnios. Charles himself and
Doria arrived safely at Bujēya—then a Spanish outpost—with part of the flotilla. Here the unexpected
visitors soon caused a famine—and still the tempest
raged. The half-starved rovers in vain tried to make
head against the waves, and carry the Emperor back
to Spain : eighty miles out they gave in, and the
ships returned disconsolately to the harbour. Twelve
days and nights the storm bellowed along the
treacherous coast, and not till November 23rd could
the Imperial fleet set sail for the coast of Spain.

There was mourning in Castile that Yuletide.
Besides eight thousand rank and file, three hundred
officers of birth had fallen victims to the storm or
the Moorish lance. Algiers teemed with Christian
captives, and it became a common saying that a
Christian slave was scarce a fair barter for an
onion

So ended this famous expedition. It was begun in
glory, and ended in shame. The whole of Christendom, one might say—for there were English knights
there, like Sir Thomas Challoner, as well as Germans,
Frenchmen, Spaniards, and Italians in the army—

had gone forth to destroy a nest of pirates, and behold, by the fury of the elements and the foolishness of their own counsels, they were almost destroyed themselves. They had left behind them ships and men and stores and cannon : worse, they had left Algiers stronger and more defiant than ever.

The Algerines, for their part, never forgot the valour of the Knights of Malta, and the spot where they made their stand is still called " The Grave of the Knights." High up on the hillside may be seen " the Emperor's Castle," which marks the traditional place where Charles' great pavilion was pitched on the morning of the fatal 23rd of October.

" The climate of Africa "—it is the caustic comment of Admiral Jurien de la Gravière—" was evidently unsuited to deeds of chivalry."

XII.

DRAGUT REÏS.

1543—1560.

THE name of Dragut has already occurred more than
once in this history: it was destined to become as
notorious as Barbarossa's as the century advanced.
Dragut—or Torghūd—was born on the Caramanian
coast opposite the island of Rhodes. Unlike many of
his colleagues he seems to have been the son of
Mohammedan parents, tillers of the earth. Being
adventurous by nature, he took service as a boy in the
Turkish fleet and became "a good pilot and a most
excellent gunner." At last he contrived to purchase
and man a galleot, with which he cruised the waters
of the Levant, where his intimate acquaintance with
all the coasts and islands enabled him to seize and
dispose of many prizes. Kheyr-ed-dīn Barbarossa
soon came to hear of his exploits, and welcomed him
heartily when he came to pay his respects at Algiers,
in so far that he gave him the conduct of various
expeditions and eventually appointed him his
lieutenant with the command of twelve galleys.
"From thenceforward this redoubtable Corsair
passed not one summer without ravaging the coasts

CASTLE OF JERBA.

(*Elisée Reclus.*)

óf Naples and Sicily : nor durst any Christian vessels
attempt to pass between Spain and Italy ; for if they
offered it, he infallibly snapped them up : and when
he missed any of his prey at sea, he made himself
amends by making descents along the coasts, plundering villages and towns, and dragging away multitudes
of inhabitants into captivity." [1]

In 1540, as we have seen, Dragut was caught by
Giannettino Doria, who made him a present to his
great kinsman Andrea, on whose galleys he was
forced to toil in chains. La Valette, afterwards Grand
Master of Malta, who had once pulled the captive's
oar on Barbarossa's ships and knew Dragut well,
one day saw the ex-Corsair straining on the galley
bank : " Señor Dragut," said he, " *usanza de guerra !*
—'tis the custom of war ! "   And the prisoner,
remembering his visitor's former apprenticeship,
replied cheerfully, " *Y mudanza de fortuna*—a change
of luck ! "   He did not lose heart, and in 1543 Barbarossa ransomed him for 3000 crowns,[2] and made him
chief of the galleys of the western Corsairs. Imprison-
ment had sharpened his appetite for Christians, and
he harried the Italian coasts with more than his
ancient zeal. Surrounded by bold spirits and commanding a fleet of his own, Dragut had the Mediterranean in his grasp, and even ventured to seize the
most dreaded of all foes, a Maltese galley, wherein he
found 70,000 ducats intended for the repair of the
fortifications of Tripoli, which then belonged to "the

[1] MORGAN, *Hist. of Algiers*, 439.
[2] BRANTÔME. *Hommes illustres étrangers.*   Oeuvres, i. 279.

Religion." As the Turkish annalist says, " Torghūd
had become the drawn sword of Islam."

Dragut's lair was at the island of Jerba, which
tradition links with the lotus-eaters, perhaps because
of the luxuriant fertility of the soil. The people of
Jerba, despite their simple agricultural pursuits, were
impatient of control, and, as often as not, were
independent of the neighbouring kingdom of Tunis or
any other state. Here, with or without their leave,
Dragut took up his position, probably in the very
castle which Roger Doria, when lord of the island,
began to build in 1289 ; and from out the wide lake
at the back the Corsair's galleots issued to ravage the
lands which were under the protection of Roger
Doria's descendants. Not content with the rich
spoils of Europe, Dragut took the Spanish outposts
in Africa, one by one—Susa, Sfax, Monastir ; and
finally set forth to conquer " Africa."

It is not uncommon in Arabic to call a country and
its capital by the same name. Thus Misr meant and
still means both Egypt and Cairo ; El-Andalus, both
Spain and Cordova. Similarly " Africa " meant to
the Arabs the province of Carthage or Tunis and its
capital, which was not at first Tunis but successively
Kayrawān and Mahdīya. Throughout the later
middle ages the name " Africa " is applied by
Christian writers to the latter city. Here it was that
in 1390 a " grand and noble enterprize " came to an
untimely end. " The Genoese," says Froissart, " bore
great enmity to this town ; for its Corsairs frequently
watched them at sea, and when strongest fell on and
plundered their ships, carrying their spoils to this

SIEGE OF "AFRICA," 1390.

(*From a MS.*)

town of Africa, which was and is now their place of
deposit and may be called their warren." It was
"beyond measure strong, surrounded by high walls,
gates, and deep ditches." The chivalry of Christendom
hearkened to the prayer of the Genoese and the people
of Majorca and Sardinia and Ischia, and the many
islands that groaned beneath the Corsairs' devasta-
tions; the Duke of Bourbon took command of an
expedition (at the cost of the Genoese) which included

GREEK FIRE.
(*From a MS.*)

names as famous as the Count d'Auvergne, the Lord
de Courcy, Sir John de Vienne, the Count of Eu, and
our own Henry of Beaufort; and on St. John Baptist's
Day, with much pomp, with flying banners and the
blowing of trumpets, they sailed on three hundred
galleys for Barbary. Arrived before Africa, not without
the hindrance of a storm, they beheld the city in the
form of a bow, reaching out its arms to the sea; high
were its ramparts; and a colossal tower, armed with

stone-projectiles, guarded the harbour. Nevertheless the Knights landed in good heart, after a cup of Grecian or Malmsey wine, on the Vigil of Magdalen Day (July 22nd), unopposed, and each great lord set

MEDIEVAL FIREARMS.
(*From a MS.*)

up his pennon before his tent over against the fortress, with the Genoese crossbows on the right. Here they remained nine weeks. The Saracens never offered battle, but harassed the enemy with their

MEDIEVAL PROJECTILES.
(*From a MS.*)

skirmishers, who fired their arrows, then dropped down behind their targets of Cappadocian leather to avoid the enemy's return volley; then, rising again, cast their javelins with deadly aim. What was to be done ? The Duke of Bourbon spent his time in sitting crosslegged before his tent ; the nobles and knights had plenty of excellent wine and food ; but it was very hot and uncomfortable—the assault had failed—many had died—the Genoese wanted to get their galleys back safe in port before the autumn gales came on ; so they packed up their baggage, and re-embarked, blowing their horns and beating their drums for very joy." [1]

This was the city which Dragut took without a blow in the spring of 1550. Mahdīya was then in an anarchic state, ruled by a council of chiefs, each ready to betray the other, and none owing the smallest allegiance to any king, least of all the despised king of Tunis, Hamīd, who had deposed and blinded his father Hasan, Charles V.'s *protégé*. One of these chiefs let Dragut and his merry men into the city by night, and the inhabitants woke up to find " Africa " in the possession of the bold Corsair whose red and white ensign, displaying a blue crescent, floated from the battlements.

So easy a triumph roused the emulation of Christendom. Where the Duke of Bourbon had failed, Dragut had conspicuously succeeded. Don Garcia de Toledo dreamed of outshining the Corsair's glory. His father, the Viceroy of Naples, the Pope, and others, promised their aid, and old Andrea Doria took the command. After much delay and consultation a large body of troops was conveyed to Mahdīya, and disembarked on June 28, 1550. Dragut,

[1] FROISSART'S *Chron.*, transl. T. Johnes (1844) ii. 446, 465, ff.

though aware of the project, was at sea, devastating the Gulf of Genoa, and paying himself in advance for any loss the Christians might inflict in Africa : his nephew, Hisār Reïs commanded in the city. When Dragut returned, the siege had gone on for a month, without result ; a tremendous assault had been repulsed with heavy loss to the besiegers, who were growing disheartened. The Corsair assembled a body of Moors and Turks and attempted to relieve the fortress ; but his ambuscade failed, Hisār's simultaneous sally was driven back, and Dragut, seeing that he could do nothing, fled to Jerba. His retreat gave fresh energy to the siege, and a change of attack discovered the weak places of the defence. A vigorous assault on the 8th of September carried the walls, a brisk street fight ensued, and the strong city of "Africa" was in the hands of the Christians.

The Sultan, Suleymān the Great, was little pleased to see a Moslem fortress summarily stormed by the troops of his ally, the Emperor. Charles replied that he had fought against pirates, not against the Sultan's vassals ; but Suleymān could not perceive the distinction, and emphasized his disapproval by giving Dragut twenty galleys, which soon found their way to Christian shores. The lamentations of his victims roused Doria, who had the good fortune to surprise the Corsair as he was greasing his keels in the strait behind Jerba. This strait was virtually a *cul-de-sac*. Between the island and the great lake that lay behind it, the sea had worn a narrow channel on the northern side, through which light vessels could pass, with care ; but to go out of the lake by the southern side involved a voyage over what was little better than a bog, and no one ever thought of the attempt. Doria saw he had his enemy in a trap, and was in no hurry to venture in among the shoals and narrows of the strait. He sent joyous messages to Europe, announcing his triumph, and cautiously, as was his habit, awaited events.

Dragut, for his part, dared not push out against a vastly superior force ; his only chance was a ruse. Accordingly, putting a bold face on the matter, he manned a small earthwork with cannon, and played upon the enemy, with little or no actual injury, beyond the all-important effect of making Doria hesitate still more. Meanwhile, in the night, while his little battery is perplexing the foe, all is prepared at the southern extremity of the strait. Summoning a couple of thousand field labourers, he sets them to work ; here a small canal is dug—there rollers come into play ; and in a few hours his small fleet is safely transported to the open water on the south side of the island. Calling off his men from the illusive battery, the Corsair is off for the Archipelago : by good luck he picks up a fine galley on the way, which was conveying news of the reinforcements coming to Doria. The old Genoese admiral never gets the message : he is rubbing his eyes in sore amazement, wondering what had happened to the imprisoned fleet. Never was admiral more cruelly cheated : never did Doria curse the nimble Corsair with greater vehemence or better cause.

Next year, 1551, Dragut's place was with the Ottoman navy, then commanded by Sinān Pasha. He

had had enough of solitary roving, and found it
almost too exciting : he now preferred to hunt in
couples. With nearly a hundred and fifty galleys or
galleots, ten thousand soldiers, and numerous siege
guns, Sinān and Dragut sailed out of the Dardanelles—
whither bound no Christian could tell. They ravaged,
as usual, the Straits of Messina, and then revealed the
point of attack by making direct for Malta. The
Knights of St. John were a perpetual thorn in the
side of the Turks, and even more vexatious to the
Corsairs, whose vessels they, and they alone, dared
to tackle single-handed, and too often with success.
Sultan and Corsair were alike eager to dislodge the
Knights from the rock which they had been fortifying
for twenty years, just as Suleymān had dislodged
them from Rhodes, which they had been fortifying
for two hundred. In July the Turkish fleet appeared
before the Marsa, wholly unexpected by the Knights.
The Turks landed on the tongue of promontory which
separates the two great harbours, and where there
was as yet no Fort St. Elmo to molest them. Sinān
was taken aback by the strong aspect of the fortress
of St. Angelo on the further side of the harbour, and
almost repented of his venture. To complete his
dejection, he seems to have courted failure. Instead
of boldly throwing his whole force upon the small
garrison and overwhelming them by sheer weight, he
tried a reconnaissance, and fell into an ambuscade ;
upon which he incontinently abandoned all thought
of a siege, and contented himself with laying waste
the interior of Malta, and taking the adjacent island
of Goza.

The quantity of booty he would bring back to Constantinople might perhaps avail, he thought, to keep his head on his shoulders, after so conspicuous a failure; but Sinān preferred not to trust to the chance. To wipe out his defeat, he sailed straight for Tripoli, some sixty-four leagues away. Tripoli was the natural antidote to Malta: for Tripoli, too, belonged to the Knights of St. John—much against their will—inasmuch as the Emperor had made their defence of this easternmost Barbary state a condition of their tenure of Malta. So far they had been unable to put it into a proper state of defence, and with crumbling battlements and a weak garrison, they had yearly expected invasion. The hour had now come. Summoned to surrender, the Commandant, Gaspard de Villiers, of the Auvergne Tongue, replied that the city had been entrusted to his charge, and he would defend it to the death. He had but four hundred men to hold the fort withal.

Six thousand Turks disembarked, forty cannons were landed, Sinān himself directed every movement, and arranged his batteries and earthworks. A heavy cannonade produced no effect on the walls, and the Turkish admiral thought of the recent repulse at Malta, and of the stern face of his master; and his head sat uneasily upon his neck. The siege appeared to make no progress. Perhaps this venture, too, would have failed, but for the treachery of a French renegade, who escaped into the trenches and pointed out the weak places in the walls. His counsel was taken; the walls fell down; the garrison, in weariness and despair, had lain down to sleep off their troubles, and no reproaches and blows could rouse them. On August 15th Gaspard de Villiers was forced to surrender, on terms, as he believed, identical with those which Suleymān granted to the Knights of Rhodes.[1] But Sinān was no Suleymān ; moreover, he was in a furious rage with the whole Order. He put the garrison—all save a few—in chains, and carried them off to grace his triumph at Stambol.

Thus did Tripoli fall once more into the hands of the Moslems, forty-one years after its conquest by the Count Don Pedro Navarro.[2]

The misfortunes of the Christians did not end here. Year after year the Ottoman fleet appeared in Italian waters, marshalled now by Sinān, and when he died by Piāli Pasha the Croat, but always with Dragut in the van ; year by year the coasts of Apulia and Calabria yielded up more and more of their treasure, their youth, and their beauty, to the Moslem ravishers ; yet worse, was in store. Unable as they felt themselves to cope with the Turks at sea, the Powers of Southern Europe resolved to strike one more blow on land, and recover Tripoli. A fleet of nearly a hundred galleys and ships, gathered from Spain, Genoa, "the Religion," the Pope, from all quarters, with the Duke de Medina-Celi at the head, assembled at Messina. Doria was too old to command, but his kinsman, Giovanni Andrea, son of his loved and lost Giannettino, led the Genoese galleys. The Fates seemed adverse from the outset. Five times the expedition put to sea ; five times was it driven back

[1] See the *Story of Turkey*, 170.
[2] See JURIEN DE LA GRAVIÈRE, *Les Corsaires Barbaresques*, 193–215.

by contrary winds.[1]   At last, on February 10, 1560,
it was fairly away for the African coast.   Here fresh
troubles awaited it.   Long delays in crowded vessels
had produced their disastrous effects: fevers and scurvy
and dysentery were working their terrible ravages
among the crews, and two thousand corpses were flung
into the sea.   It was impossible to lay siege to Tripoli
with a diseased army, and when actually in sight of
their object the admirals gave orders to return to Jerba.

A sudden descent quickly gave them the command
of the beautiful island.   The Arab sheykh whose
people cultivated it was as ready to pay tribute to
the Spaniard as to the Corsair.   Medina-Celi and
his troops accordingly set to work undisturbed at
the erection of a fortress strong enough to baffle
the besieging genius even of the Turks.   In two
months a strong castle was built, with all scientific
earthworks, and the admiral prepared to carry home
such troops as were not needed for its defence.

Unhappily for him, he had lingered too long.   He
had wished to see the defences complete, and had
trusted to the usual practice of the Turks, not to put
to sea before May was advanced.   He was about to
prepare for departure when news came that the
Turkish fleet had been seen at Goza.   Instantly all
was panic.   Valiant gentlemen forgot their valour,
forgot their coolness, forgot how strong a force by
sea or land they mustered : one thought alone was
uppermost—the Turks were upon them !   Giovanni
Doria hurried on board and embarked his Genoese ;
Medina-Celi more methodically and with something

[1] *Les Corsaires Barbaresques*, 266.

like *sang froid* personally supervised the embarcation
of his men ; but before they could make out of the
strait, where Dragut had so narrowly escaped capture,
the dread Corsair himself, and Ochiali, and Piāli
Pasha were upon them. Then ensued a scene of
confusion that baffles description. Despairing of
weathering the north side of Jerba the panic-stricken
Christians ran their ships ashore, and deserted them,
never stopping even to set them on fire. The deep-
draught galleons stuck fast in the shallow water. On
rowed the Turks ; galleys and galleons to the number
of fifty-six fell into their hands ; eighteen thousand
Christians bowed down before their scimitars ; the
beach, on that memorable 11th of May, 1560, was a
confused medley of stranded ships, helpless prisoners,
Turks busy in looting men and galleys—and a hideous
heap of mangled bodies. The fleet and the army
which had sailed from Messina but three months ago
in such gallant array were absolutely lost. It was a
dies nefas for Christendom.

Medina-Celi and young Doria made good their
escape by night. But when the old Genoese admiral
learnt the terrible news, the loss of the fleet he loved,
the defeat of the nephew he loved yet more, his dim
eyes were wet. "Take me to the church," he said ;
and he soon received the last consolations of religion.
Long as he had lived, and many as had been the vicis-
situdes of his great career, he had willingly been spared
this last most miserable experience. On November 25,
1560, he gave up the ghost : he was a great seaman, but
still more a passionate lover of his country ;—despotic
in his love, but not the less a noble Genoese patriot.

XIII.

THE KNIGHTS OF MALTA.

1565.

WHEN Sultan Suleymān reflected on the magnanimity which he had displayed towards the Knights of Rhodes in allowing them to depart in peace in 1522, his feelings must have resembled those of Doria when he thought of that inconsiderate release of Dragut in 1543. Assuredly the royal clemency had been ill-rewarded ; the Knights had displayed a singular form of gratitude to the sparer of their lives ; they had devoted themselves to him, indeed, but devoted themselves to his destruction. The cavaliers whom Charles V. suffered to perch on the glaring white rock of Malta, in 1530, proved in no long time to be a pest as virulent and all-pervading as even Rhodes had harboured. Seven galleys they owned, and never more, but the seven were royal vessels, splendidly armed and equipped, and each a match for two or three Turkish ships.[1] Every year they cruised from Sicily to the Levant, and many a prize laden

---

[1] See an excellent account of the galleys and discipline of the Knights of St. John in JURIEN DE LA GRAVIÈRE, *les Derniers Jours de la Marine à Rames*, ch. ix. ; and *Les Chevaliers de Malte*, tome i.

with precious store they carried off to Malta. The commerce of Egypt and Syria was in danger of annihilation ; the Barbary Corsairs, even Dragut himself, shunned a meeting with the red galleys of " the Religion," or their black *capitana ;* and the Turkish fleet, while holding undisputed sway over the Mediterranean, was not nimble enough to surprise the Maltese squadron in its rapid and incalculable expeditions. Jean de la Valette Parisot, General of the Galleys and afterwards Grand Master, Francis of Lorraine, Grand Prior of France, Romegas, prince of knights-errant, scoured the seas in search of prey : —they were as true pirates as ever weathered the " white squall." The Knights lived by plunder as much as any Corsair ; but they tempered their free-booting with chivalry and devotions ; they were the protectors of the helpless and afflicted, and they preyed chiefly upon the enemies of the Faith.

Meanwhile they built and built ; Fort St. Elmo rose on the central promontory, Forts St. Michael and St. Angelo were strengthened ; bastions were skilfully planned, flanking angles devised, ravelins and cavaliers erected, ditches deepened, parapets raised, embrasures opened, and every device of sixteenth-century fortification as practised by Master Evangelista, chief engineer of the Order, was brought into use. For the Knights knew that Suleymān lived and was mightier than ever. Their cruisers had wrought sad havoc among his subjects, and the Sultan would not long suffer the hornets of Rhodes to swarm at Malta. They lived in constant expectation of attack, and they spent all their strength and all their money in preparing for the day of the Sultan's revenge. At last the time came: Suleymān swore in his wrath that the miscreants should no longer defy him ; he had suffered them to leave Rhodes as gentlemen of honour—he would consume them in Malta as one burns a nest of wasps.

At the time of the siege of 1565 the city or fortress of Malta was situated, not as Valetta now stands on the west, but on the east side of the Marsa or great harbour. To understand even the briefest narrative of one of the most heroic deeds of war that the world has seen, the position of the forts must be understood. (See the Plan.) On the northern coast of the rocky island a bold promontory or rugged tongue of land, Mount Sceberras, separates two deep bights or inlets. The eastern of these was called Marsa Muset, or "Middle Port," but was unoccupied and without defences at the time of the siege, except that the guns of St. Elmo, the fortress at the point of the Sceberras promontory, commanded its mouth. The Marsa Kebir, or simply La Marsa, the "Great Port," was the chief stronghold of the Knights. Here four projecting spits of rock formed smaller harbours on the western side. The outermost promontory, the Pointe des Fourches, separated the Port de la Renelle or La Arenela, from the open sea ; Cape Salvador divided the Arenela from the English Harbour ; the Burg, the main fortress and capital of the place, with Fort St. Angelo at its point, shot out between the English Harbour and the Harbour of the Galleys ; and the Isle of La Sangle, joined by a sandy isthmus to the mainland, and crowned by Fort St. Michael,

severed the Galley Harbour from that of La Sangle.
All round these inlets high hills dominated the ports.
Behind Fort St. Elmo, the Sceberras climbed steeply
to a considerable height. Behind the Arenela and
English Harbour rose Mount Salvador, Calcara, and
further back the Heights of St. Catherine. The
Burg and Fort St. Michael were overtopped by the
Heights of St. Margaret, whilst the Conradin plateau
looked down upon the head of the Marsa and
the Harbour of La Sangle. To modern artillery
and engineering the siege would have been easy,
despite the rocky hardness of the ground, since the
Knights had not had time to construct those field-
works upon the surrounding heights which were
essential to the safety of the forts. Even to the
skilled but undeveloped artillery of the Turks, the
destruction of Malta ought not to have been either a
difficult or lengthy operation, had they begun at the
right place.

To those who were acquainted with the ground,
who had heard of the siege of Rhodes, and knew that
the Turks were not less but more formidable in 1565
than in 1522, the issue of the struggle must have
appeared inevitable, when the huge Ottoman fleet
hove in view on the 18th of May, 1565. One hundred
and eighty vessels, of which two-thirds were galleys-
royal, carried more than thirty thousand fighting
men—the pick of the Ottoman army, tried Janissaries
and Sipāhis, horsemen from Thrace, rough warriors
from the mountains of Anatolia, eager volunteers
from all parts of the Sultan's dominions. Mustafa
Pasha who had grown old in the wars of his master,

commanded on land, and Piāli was admiral of the fleet.
Dragut was to join them immediately, and the Sultan's
order was that nothing should be done till he arrived.

The Knights had not remained ignorant of the
preparations that were making against them. They
sent to all Europe for help, and the Pope gave money,
and Spain promises: the Viceroy of Sicily would send
Spanish reinforcements by the 15th of June. They
worked unceasingly at their defences and did all that
men could do to meet the advancing storm. All
told, they mustered but seven hundred Knights, and
between eight and nine thousand mercenaries of
various nations, but chiefly Maltese, who could only
be trusted behind walls.

The Order was fortunate in its Grand Master.
Jean de la Valette, born in 1494, a Knight of St.
John before he was of age, and a defender of Rhodes
forty-three years ago, though now an old man re-
tained to the full the courage and generalship which
had made his career as commander of the galleys
memorable in the annals of Mediterranean wars. He
had been a captive among the Turks, and knew their
languages and their modes of warfare; and his
sufferings had increased his hatred of the Infidel. A
tall, handsome man, with an air of calm resolution, he
communicated his iron nerve to all his followers.
Cold and even cruel in his severity, he was yet
devoutly religious, and passionately devoted to his
Order and his Faith. A true hero, but of the
reasoning, merciless, bigoted sort: not the generous,
reckless enthusiast who inspires by sympathy and
glowing example.

11

When he knew that the day of trial was at hand, Jean de la Valette assembled the Order together, and bade them first be reconciled with God and one another, and then prepare to lay down their lives for the Faith they had sworn to defend. Before the altar each Knight foreswore all enmities, renounced all pleasures, buried all ambitions; and joining together in the sacred fellowship of the Supper of the Lord, once more dedicated their blood to the service of the Cross.

At the very outset a grave mischance befell the Turks; Dragut was a fortnight late at the rendezvous. His voice would have enforced Piāli's advice, to land the entire force and attack the Burg and St. Michael from the heights behind. Mustafa, the Seraskier, was determined to reduce the outlying Fort of St. Elmo on the promontory of Sceberras before attacking the main position, and accordingly landed his men at his convenience from the Marsa Muset, and laid out his earthworks on the land side of St. Elmo. He had not long begun when Ochiali arrived with six galleys from Alexandria, and on June 2nd came Dragut himself with a score or more galleys of Tripoli and Bona. Dragut saw at once the mistake that had been made, but saw also that to abandon the siege of St. Elmo would too greatly elate the Knights: the work must go on; and on it went with unexampled zeal.

The little fort could hold but a small garrison, but the force was a *corps d'élite :* De Broglio of Piedmont commanded it with sixty soldiers, and was supported by Juan de Guaras, bailiff of the Negropont, a splendid old Knight, followed by sixty more of the

Order, and some Spaniards under Juan de la Cerda :—
a few hundred of men to meet thirty thousand Turks,
but men of no common mettle. They had not long
to wait. The fire opened from twenty-one guns on
the last day of May and continued with little intermission till June 23rd. The besiegers were confident
of battering down the little fort in a week at most,
but they did not know their foes. As soon as one
wall crumbled before the cannonade, a new work
appeared behind it. The first assault lasted three
hours, and the Turks gained possession of the
ravelin in front of the gate ; so furious was the onset
that the defenders sent to the Grand Master to tell
him the position was untenable ; they could not stand
a second storming party. La Valette replied that, if
so, he would come and withstand it himself : St. Elmo
must be held to keep the Turks back till reinforcements arrived. So of course they went on. Dragut
brought up some of his largest yards and laid them
like a bridge across the fosse, and a tremendous
struggle raged for five terrible hours on Dragut's
bridge. Again and again Mustafa marshalled his
Janissaries for the attack, and every time they were
hurled back with deadly slaughter. As many as four
thousand Turks fell in a single assault. St. Elmo
was little more than a heap of ruins, but the garrison
still stood undaunted among the heaps of stones,
each man ready to sell his life dearly for the honour
of Our Lady and St. John.

The Turks at last remedied the mistake they had
made at the beginning. They had left the communi-
cation between St. Elmo and the harbour unimpeded,

and reinforcements had frequently been introduced into the besieged fortress from the Burg. On June 17th the line of circumvallation was pushed to the harbour's edge, and St. Elmo was completely isolated. Yet this prudent precaution was more than outweighed by the heavy loss that accompanied its execution : for Dragut was struck down while directing the engineers, and the surgeons pronounced the wound mortal. With the cool courage of his nation, Mustafa cast a cloak over the prostrate form, and stood in Dragut's place.

Five days later came the final assault. On the eve of June 23rd, after the cannonade had raged all the forenoon, and a hand-to-hand fight had lasted till the evening, when two thousand of the enemy and five hundred of the scanty garrison had fallen, the Knights and their soldiers prepared for the end. They knew the Grand Master could not save them, that nothing could avert the inevitable dawn. They took the Sacrament from each other's hands, and "committing their souls to God made ready to devote their bodies in the cause of His Blessed Son." It was a forlorn and sickly remnant of the proudest chivalry the world has ever known, that met the conquering Turks that June morning : worn and haggard faces, pale with long vigils and open wounds ; tottering frames that scarce could stand ; some even for very weakness seated in chairs, with drawn swords, within the breach. But weary and sick, upright or seated, all bore themselves with unflinching courage ; in every set face was read the resolve to die hard.

The ghastly struggle was soon over : the weight of the Turkish column bore down everything in its furious rush. Knights and soldiers alike rolled upon the ground, every inch of which they had disputed to the last drop of their blood. Not a man escaped.

Dragut heard of the fall of St. Elmo as he lay in his tent dying, and said his Moslem *Nunc Dimittis* with a thankful heart. He had been struck at the soldier's post of duty ; he died with the shout of victory ringing in his ears, as every general would wish to die. His figure stands apart from all the men of his age :—an admiral, the equal of Barbarossa, the superior of Doria ; a general fit to marshal troops against any of the great leaders of the armies of Charles V. ; he was content with the eager rush of his life, and asked not for sovereignty or honours. Humane to his prisoners, a gay comrade, an inspiriting commander, a seaman every inch, Dragut is the most vivid and original personage among the Corsairs.

St. Elmo had fallen : but St. Angelo and St. Michael stood untouched. Three hundred Knights of St. John and thirteen hundred soldiers had indeed fallen in the first, but its capture had closed the lives of eight thousand Turks. "If the child has cost us so dear," said Mustafa, "what will the parent cost ?" The Turkish general sent a flag of truce to La Valette, to propose terms of capitulation, but in vain. Mutual animosity had been worked to a height of indignant passion by a barbarous massacre of prisoners on both sides, each in view of the other. The Grand Master's first impulse was to hang the messenger of such foes ; he thought better of it, and showed him the depth of the ditch that encircled the twin forts : "Let your Janissaries come and take that," he said, and contemptuously dismissed him.

A new siege now began. The forts on the east of La Marsa had been sorely drained to fill up the gaps in the garrison at St. Elmo, and it was fortunate that Don Juan de Cardona had been able to send a reinforcement, though only of six hundred men, under Melchior de Robles, to the Old Town, whence they contrived to reach Fort St. Michael in safety.[1] Even six hundred men added materially to the difficulties of the siege : for, be it remembered, six hundred men behind skilfully constructed fortifications may be worth six thousand in the open. It was very hard for the besiegers to find cover. The ground was hard rock, and cutting trenches was extremely arduous work, and the noise of the picks directed the fire of the forts by night upon the sappers. Nevertheless by July 5th four batteries were playing upon St. Michael from the heights of St. Margaret and Conradin, while the guns of Fort St. Elmo opened from the other side ; and soon a line of cannon on Mount Salvador dominated the English Port. An attempt to bring a flotilla of gunboats into the Harbour of the Galleys failed, after a vigorous conflict between a party of Turkish swimmers, who strove with axes to cut the chain that barred the port, and some Maltese who swam to oppose them, sword in teeth. The battle in the water ended in the flight of the Turks.

[1] Jurien de la Gravière, *Les Chevaliers de Malte et la Marine de Philippe II.*, ii. 71.

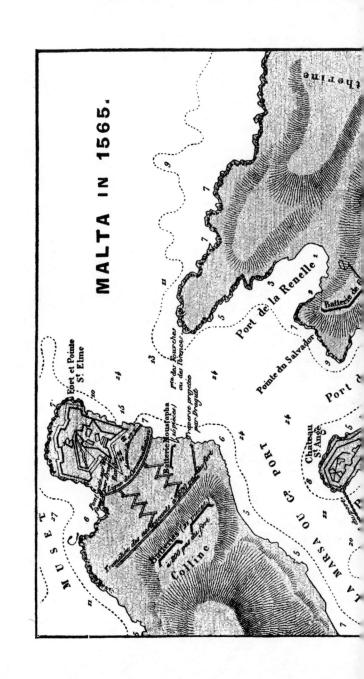

MALTA IN 1565.

SKETCH OF THE PORT OF MALTA IN 1565.

(*Jurien de la Gravière.*)

Ten distinct general assaults were delivered with all the fury of Janissaries against the stronghold. First, a grand assault by sea was ordered on July 15th. Three columns simultaneously advanced by night on Fort St. Michael : one landed in the Arenela and marched to attack the eastern suburb La Bormula ; the second came down from the heights of St. Margaret and made straight for the bastion defended by De Robles ; the third advanced from Conradin on the south-west, and assaulted the salient angle at the extreme point of the spit of land on which the fort was built. In vain the Turks swarmed up the scaling-ladders ; company after company was hurled down, a huddled mass of mangled flesh, and the ladders were cast off. Again the escalade began :— the Knights rolled huge blocks of masonry on the crowded throng below ; when they got within arms' reach the scimitar was no match for the long two-handed swords of the Christians. At all three points after a splendid attack, which called forth all the finest qualities of the magnificent soldiery of Suleymān the Great, the Turks were repulsed with terrible loss. The Knights lost some of their bravest swords, and each one of them fought like a lion : but their dead were few compared with the unfortunate troops of Barbary, who had cut off their retreat by dismissing their ships, and were slaughtered or drowned in the harbour by hundreds. The water was red with their blood, and mottled with standards and drums and floating robes. Of prisoners, the Christians spared but two, and these they delivered over to the mob to be torn in pieces.

After the assault by water came the attack by
mines ; but the result was no better, for the Knights
were no novices in the art of countermining, and the
attempt to push on after the explosion ended in
rushing into a trap. Mustafa, however, continued to
work underground and ply his heavy artillery, with
hardly a pause, upon the two extremities of the line
of landward defences—the Bastion of De Robles, and
the Bastion of Castile : both were in ruins by the
27th of July, as Sālih Reïs, son of Barbarossa's old
comrade, satisfied himself by a reconnaissance pushed
into the very breach. An assault was ordered
for midday of August 2nd, when the Christians
were resting after the toils of the sultry morning.
Six thousand Turks advanced in absolute silence
to Melchior de Robles' bastion ; they had almost
reached their goal when the shout of the sentry
brought that gallant Knight, readily awakened,
to the breach, followed by Muñatones and three
Spanish arquebusiers. These five warriors held
twenty-six Janissaries and Sipāhis in check till reinforcements came ; and they killed fifteen of them.
Their valour saved the fort. Four hours longer the
struggle lasted, till neither party could deal another
blow in the raging August sun ; and the Turks at
last retired with a loss of six hundred dead.

Nothing daunted, the 7th of August saw them once
more scaling the walls and rushing the breaches of the
two bastions, this time with nearly twenty thousand
men. They poured over the ravelin, swarmed up the
breach, and were on the point of carrying the fort.
All was nearly lost, and at that supreme moment even

the aged Grand Master, whose place was to direct, not to imperil his life, came down to the front of battle, and used his sword and pike like a common soldier. Eight long hours they fought, six times came fresh reserves to the support of the Turks ; the Christians were exhausted, and had no reserves. One rush more and the place would be carried.

Just then a body of cavalry was seen riding down from the direction of the Old Town. The Turks took them to be the long-expected reinforcements from Sicily. They are seen to fall upon stray parties of Turks ; they must be the advance guard of Philip's army. Piāli in alarm runs to his galleys ; the Turks who had all but carried the long-contested bastion pause in affright lest they be taken in rear. In vain Mustafa, in vain the King of Algiers shows them that the horsemen are but two hundred of the Old Town garrison, with no army at all behind them. Panic, unreasoning and fatal as ever, seizes upon the troops : the foothold won after eight hours of furious fighting is surrendered to a scare ; not a Turk stays to finish the victory. The lives of their two thousand dead need not have been sacrificed.

Still Mustafa did not despair. He knew that the main defences of the bastions had been destroyed—a few days more, a heavy cannonade, the explosion of a series of mines which thousands of his sappers were preparing would, he was certain, ensure the success of a final assault. The day came, August 20th, and Mustafa himself, in his coat of inlaid mail and robe of cramoisy, led his army forward ; but a well-directed fire drove him into a trench, whence he emerged not

till night covered his path.   When at last he got back,
he found his army in camp ; another assault had been
repulsed.   The next day they went up again to the fatal
embrasures, and this time the failure was even more
signal ; repeated repulses were telling on the spirits
of the men, and the veteran Janissaries went to their
work with unaccustomed reluctance.   Nevertheless, the
trenches, cut in the hard rock, continued to advance
slowly, and the cavalier behind the ravelin was taken
after a severe struggle :—just taken, when La Valette's
mines blew the victorious assailants into the air.   On
the 30th another well-planned assault was repelled.
One more effort—a last and desperate attempt—was
to be made on the 7th of September ; but on the 5th
the news arrived that the Spanish army of relief had
at length, after inconceivable delays and hesitations,
actually landed on the island.   The worn-out Turks
did not wait to reconnoitre, they had borne enough : a
retreat was ordered, the siege was abandoned, the
works that had cost so much labour and blood were
deserted, and there was a general stampede to the
galleys.   It is true they landed again when they learnt
that the relieving army numbered but six thousand
men ; but their strength was departed from them.
They tried to fight the relieving army, and then again
they ran for the ships.   The Spaniards cut them down
like sheep, and of all that gallant armament scarce
five thousand lived to tell the tale of those terrible
three months in Malta.

No more moving sight can be imagined than the
meeting of the new-come Brethren of the Order and
their comrades of St. Michael's Fort.   The worn

remnant of the garrison, all told, was scarcely six hundred strong, and hardly a man was without a wound. The Grand Master and his few surviving Knights looked like phantoms from another world, so pale and grisly were they, faint from their wounds, their hair and beard unkempt, their armour stained, and neglected, as men must look who had hardly slept without their weapons for more than three memorable months. As they saw these gaunt heroes the rescuers burst into tears; strangers clasped hands and wept together with the same overpowering emotion that mastered relievers and relieved when Havelock and Colin Campbell led the Highlanders into Lucknow. Never surely had men deserved more nobly the homage of mankind. In all history there is no record of such a siege, of such a disproportion in the forces, of such a glorious outcome. The Knights of Malta live for ever among the heroes of all time.

XIV.

LEPANTO.

1571.

THE failure of the siege of Malta was a sensible rebuff, yet it cannot be said that it seriously injured the renown of the Turks in the Mediterranean. They had been resisted on land; they had not yet been beaten at sea. Nor could they look back on the terrible months of the siege without some compensating feeling of consolation. They had taken St. Elmo, and its fall had aroused general jubilation in every Moslem breast; the Moors of Granada went near to rising against the Spaniards on the mere report of this triumph of the Turkish arms. Though they had failed to reduce St. Michael, the cause was to be found, at least in part, in a false alarm and an unreasoning panic. To be defeated by such warriors as the Knights of St. John was not a disgrace; like the Highlanders in the Crimean War, these men were not so much soldiers, in their opponents' eyes, as veritable devils; and who shall contend against the legions of the Jinn? Moreover, forced as they were to abandon the siege, had they not left the island a

desert, its people reduced by half, its fortifications
heaps of rubbish, its brave defenders a handful of
invalids ?

So reasoned the Turks, and prepared for another
campaign. They had lost many men, but more were
ready to take their place ; their immense fleet was
uninjured ; and though Dragut was no more, Ochiali
—as the Christians called 'Ali *El-Ulūji* " the Renegade "—the Turks dubbed him *Fartās,* " Scurvied,"
from his complaint—was following successfully in his
old master's steps. Born at Castelli (Licastoli) in
Calabria about 1508,[1] Ochiali was to have been a
priest, but his capture by the Turks turned him to
the more exciting career of a Corsair. Soon after
the siege of Malta he succeeded Barbarossa's son
Hasan as pasha or Beglerbeg of Algiers (1568), and
one of his first acts was to retake Tunis (all but the
Goletta) in the name of Sultan Selīm II., who, to the
unspeakable loss of the Mohammedan world, had in
1566 succeeded his great father Suleymān. In July,
1570, off Alicata, on the southern coast of Sicily, Ochiali
surrounded four galleys of " the Religion "—they
then possessed but five—and took three of them, including the flag-ship, which Saint-Clément, the general of
the galleys, abandoned in order to throw himself and his
treasure on shore at Montichiaro. One galley alone,
the *St. Ann,* made a desperate resistance ; the others
surrendered. Sixty Knights or Serving Brothers of
the Order were killed or made prisoners on this
disastrous day, and so intense was the indignation in

[1] H. DE GRAMMONT, *La course, l'esclavage, et la redemption ; Un
pacha d Alger ; Hist. d'Algérie.*

Malta, that the Grand Master had much ado to save Saint-Clément from being lynched by the mob, and was obliged to deliver him up to the secular court, which at once condemned him to death. He was strangled in his cell, and his body thrown in a sack into the sea. Such a success went far to atone for Mustafa Pasha's unfortunate siege.

A far more important triumph awaited the Turks in 1570–1 :—a siege, and a conquest. The new Sultan, like his father, saw in the island of Cyprus a standing affront to his authority in the Levant. Then, as now, Cyprus was a vital centre in all maritime wars in the Eastern Mediterranean ; a convenient depôt for troops and stores ; a watch-tower whence the movements of the Turkish fleet could be observed ; a refuge for the numberless Christian Corsairs that infested the coast of Syria. Cyprus belonged to Venice, and on the score of her protection of piracy the Sultan found no difficulty in picking a quarrel with the Senate. War was declared, and Piāli Pasha transported a large army under Lala Mustafa (not the Seraskier who commanded at Malta) to lay siege to Nicosia, the capital of the island. After forty-eight days, the city fell, September 9th, and became a shambles. The catastrophe might have been averted, had the Christian fleet owned a single competent chief ; but unhappily the relief of Cyprus was entrusted to the least trustworthy of all instruments—a coalition.

Pope Pius V., a man of austere piety, full of the zeal of his high office, and in energy and intellect a born leader, spared no effort to support the Venetians as soon as war became inevitable. Few of the states

of Europe found it convenient to respond to his
appeal, but Philip of Spain sent a numerous fleet
under Giovanni Andrea Doria, and the Pope himself,
aided in some degree by the Italian princes, added
an important contingent, which he confided to the
care of the Grand Constable of Naples, Mark Antony
Colonna. Giovanni Zanne commanded the Venetian
fleet. The whole force, when united, amounted to no
less than two hundred and six vessels, of which eleven
were galleasses, and nearly all the rest galleys ; while
the soldiers and crews numbered forty-eight thousand
men. So dire was the dread then inspired by the
Turks that this vast armament dared not move
till it was known that Ochiali had left the neighbour-
hood of Italy, and even then the rivalries of the
different admirals tended rather to war between the
contingents than an attack upon the enemy's fleet.
While the Christians were wrangling, and Doria was
displaying the same Fabian caution that had led his
grand-uncle to lose the battle of Prevesa, Piāli Pasha,
wholly regardless of danger, had bared his galleys
almost entirely of soldiers, in order to aid Lala
Mustafa in the final assault on Nicosia. Had the
allied fleets attacked him on the 8th or 9th of
September it is doubtful whether a single Turkish
galley could have shown fight. But Colonna and
Doria wasted their time in wrangling and discussing,
while the foe lay powerless at their feet. Finally
they sailed back to Sicily, for fear of bad weather.
Such were the admirals who furnished the gibes of
Ochiali and his brother Corsairs. Famagusta surrendered August 4, 1571, and despite the promise of

life and liberty, the garrison was massacred and the Venetian commander, Bragadino, cruelly burnt to death. Cyprus became a Turkish possession thenceforward to this day.

Meanwhile, the Turkish and Barbary fleets, commanded by 'Ali Pasha, the successor of Piāli, and Ochiali, ravaged Crete and other islands, and coasting up the Adriatic, worked their will upon every town or village it suited their pleasure to attack. Thousands of prisoners, and stores and booty of every description rewarded their industry. At length, in September, they anchored in the Gulf of Lepanto. They had heard that the united Christian fleets were on the move, and nothing would suit the victors of Cyprus better than a round encounter with the enemy. Flushed with success, they had no fear for the issue.

Many a Christian fleet had gathered its members together before then in the waters of the Adriatic. The great battle off Prevesa was in the memory of many an old sailor as the galleys came to the rendezvous in the autumn of 1571. But there was an essential difference between then and now. Prevesa was lost by divided counsels; at Lepanto there was but one commander-in-chief. Pope Pius V. had laboured unceasingly at the task of uniting the Allies and smoothing away jealousies, and he had succeeded in drawing the navies of Southern Europe on to another year's campaign; then, warned by what he had learned of the wranglings off Cyprus, he exerted his prerogative as Vicar of God, and named as the sole commander-in-chief of the whole fleet, Don John of Austria.

ENGAGEMENT BETWEEN A SPANISH GALLEON AND A DUTCH SHIP.

(*Jurien de la Gravière.*)

Son of the most illustrious monarch of the age, Don John was born to greatness. His mother was the beautiful singer, Barba Blomberg ; his father was Charles V. The one gave him grace and beauty ; the other, the genius of command. He was but twenty-two when his half-brother, Philip, confided to him the difficult task of suppressing the rebellion of the Moors in the Alpuxarras.[1] Where the experienced veterans of Spain had failed, the beardless general of twenty-two succeeded to admiration. And now, two years later, he was called to the command of the whole navy of Southern Europe. He accepted the post with joy. He had all the hopeful confidence of youth, and he longed to fight one of the world's great battles. His enthusiasm glowed in his face : one sees it in his portraits and on the medals struck to commemorate his victory. "Beau comme un Apollon, il avait tout le prestige d'un archange envoyé par le Seigneur pour exterminer les ennemis de la Foi."

Squadron after squadron begins to crowd the Straits of Messina. Veniero, the Venetian admiral, is already there with forty-eight galleys, and sixty more expected, when Colonna enters, in July, with eighteen vessels and moors alongside. Don John has not yet arrived. He has had much ado to get his squadron ready, for no nation understands better than the Spanish the virtue of the adage *festina lente.* At last he puts off from Barcelona, and laboriously crosses the Gulf of Lyons. One may smile now at the transit, but in those days, what with the mistral

[1] See *The Story of the Moors in Spain*, p. 278.

and the risk of Corsairs, to cross the Gulf of Lyons
was a thing to be thought about. At Genoa Don
John is entertained by G. Andrea Doria, and attends
a fancy ball in a gay humour that becomes his youth
and buoyancy with all his perils still ahead. As he
proceeds, he hears how the Turks are laying waste
Dalmatia, and how the Allies are quarrelling at
Messina, but he hastens not : he knows that a galley
on a long voyage has as much a fixed pace as a horse,
and that flogging is of no use except for a short
course. At Naples he reverently receives the standard
blessed by his Holiness himself, and on August 23rd
he joins the fleet at Messina. Time is still needed
for the other ships to come up, and for the commander-in-chief to mature his plans ; before they
start, each captain of a galley will have a separate
written order, showing him his place during the
voyage and his post in any engagement, whereby the
risk of confusion and hasty marshalling is almost
done away. On the 16th of September the signal
is given to weigh anchor. Don John is off first, in
his *Reale*, a splendid *capitana* galley of sixty oars,
with a poop carved with allegorical designs by
Vasquez of Seville. After him come two hundred
and eighty-five vessels, comprising six galleasses and
two hundred and nine galleys, carrying twenty-nine
thousand men, and commanded by the most famous
names of the great families of Spain, Genoa, Venice,
Naples, Rome, Vicenza, Padua, Savoy, and Sicily.[1]
Don Juan de Cardona leads the van with seven galleys ;

[1] See the complete list in GIROLAMO CATENA, *Vita del gloriosissimo
Papa Pio Quinto*, 1587.

ARABIC ASTROLABE.

ARABIC ASTROLABE.

Don John himself, between Marcantonio Colonna and Veniero, commands the centre of sixty-two large galleys; G. A. Doria has fifty in the right wing; Barbarigo of Venice fifty-three in the left; Don Alvaro de Bazan commands the reserve of thirty galleys: the galleasses are ranged before the lines, each with five hundred arquebusiers on board. After ten days rowing and sailing they reach Corfu, and the castle greets them with thunders of joy-guns, for the fear of the Turk is removed.

'Ali Pasha, hard by in the Gulf of Lepanto, sent out scouts to ascertain the enemy's strength. A bold Barbary Corsair pushed his bark unseen by night among the Christian galleys, but his report was imperfect, and till the day of conflict neither side knew the exact strength of his opponent. The Turkish fleet numbered about two hundred and eight galleys and sixty-six galleots, and carried twenty-five thousand men. Constantinople furnished ninety-five galleys; twenty-one came from Alexandria, twenty-five from Anatolia, ten from Rhodes, ten from Mitylene, nine from Syria, twelve from Napoli di Romania, thirteen from the Negropont, and eleven from Algiers and Tripoli. The galleots were chiefly Barbary vessels, more useful for piracy than a set battle.

The two fleets unexpectedly came in sight of each other at seven o'clock on the morning of October 7th, at a point just south of the Echinades, and between Ithaca and the Gulf of Patras or Lepanto. A white sail or two on the horizon was descried by Don John's look-out on the maintop; then sail after sail rose above the sea-line, and the

enemy came into full view. Don John quickly ran
up a white flag, the signal of battle, and immediately
the whole fleet was busily engaged in clewing up the
sails to the yards, and making all snug for the conflict. The central banks were removed to make
room for the soldiers, and the slaves were served with
meat and wine. Old seamen, who had met the Turks
again and again from their youth up, prepared grimly
for revenge; sanguine boys, who held arms in set
fight for the first time that day, looked forward
eagerly to the moment of action. Even to the last
the incurable vacillation of the allied admirals was
felt: they suggested a council of war. Don John's
reply was worthy of him: "The time for councils is
past," he said; "do not trouble yourselves about aught
but fighting." Then he entered his gig, and went
from galley to galley, passing under each stern,
crucifix in hand, encouraging the men. His calm and
confident mien, and the charm of his address, excited
universal enthusiasm, and he was met on all hands
with the response: "Ready, Sir; and the sooner the
better!" Then Don John unfurled the Blessed
Standard with the figure of the Saviour, and falling
on his knees commended his cause to God.

About eleven o'clock a dead calm set in. The
Turks shortened sail and took to their oars: in perfect
order and with matchless speed and precision they
formed in line of battle, while drums and fifes announced their high spirits. The Christian fleet was
slower in falling into line; some of the galleys and
most of the galleasses were behindhand. Don John
let drop some pious oaths, and sent swift vessels

to hurry them up. At last they began to get into order. Barbarigo, the " left guide," hugged the coast with the left wing ; Don John with the centre *corps de battaille* kept touch with him ; but where was the " right guide"? Giovanni Doria, infected with the tactical vanity of his family, resolved to show these landsmen how a sailor can manoeuvre. Conceiving that Ochiali, on the Ottoman left, was trying to out-flank the Christian fleet, he bore out to sea in order to turn him. In vain Don John sent to recall him ; he had gone out of reach, and the battle had to be fought without the right wing. Doria's precious manoeuvring went near to losing the day.

The Ottoman fleet was marshalled in the same order as the Christian, except that there were no galleasses. The line of battle, nearly a mile long, was divided into centre, and right and left wing, and behind the centre was the reserve. Mohammed Shaluk (called by Europeans Scirocco) commanded the right wing, opposed to Barbarigo's left ; 'Ali Pasha opposed Don John in the centre ; Ochiali was over against the post where Doria should have been. Between the two lines stood forth the heavy galleasses, like great breakwaters, turning aside and dividing the flowing rush of the Ottoman galleys. The fire of these huge floating castles nearly caused a panic among the Turks, but they soon pulled past them, and a general melley ensued. In the Christian left, after a deadly struggle, in which both Barbarigo and Sirocco lost their lives, the Turks were repulsed, and, deprived of their chief, took to the shore, but not before the Christians had lost many galleys and a

BC—G

host of brave men. Soon after the left had been engaged, the centre came into action. 'Ali Pasha made straight for Don John's *Reale*, and his beak rammed it as far in as the fourth bank of . oars. Close by were Pertev Pasha and the *capitanas* of Colonna and Veniero. The ships became entangled, and formed one large platform of war. Twice the Spaniards of the *Reale* boarded the *Fanal* of 'Ali Pasha as far as the mainmast, and twice they were driven back with terrible loss. 'Ali himself was preparing to leap upon Don John's galley when Colonna rammed him on the poop, penetrating as far as the third oar, and delivered a withering fire from his arquebuses. The Christians had all the advantage of armour and firearms, and fired behind bulwarks; the Turks were unprotected by cuirass or helmet or bulwark, and most of them had bows instead of guns. Colonna's volleys decided the fate of the *Fanal*, and 'Ali Pasha departed this life. An hour and a half had sufficed to disperse the Ottoman right and to overpower the flagship in chief. When the fleet saw the Christian ensign at the peak of the Turkish *capitana* they redoubled their efforts: Veniero, severely wounded, still fought with the Seraskier Pertev Pasha; the Turks fled, and Pertev took to the land. In half an hour more Don John's centre was completely victorious. Then a new danger arose: Ochiali, seeing that Doria was well away to sea, sharply doubled back with all the right wing, and bore down upon the exhausted centre. He rushed upon the *capitana* of Malta, and massacred every soul on board. Dragut is avenged! Juan de

Cardona hastened to the rescue, and of his five hundred soldiers but fifty escaped; on the *Fiorenza* seventeen men alone remained alive; and other terrible losses were incurred in the furious encounter. Upon this the ingenious Doria perceived that he had outwitted only his own cause, and at last turned back. The Marquis de Santa Cruz was already upon the enemy; Don John was after him with twenty galleys; Ochiali was outnumbered, and after a brilliant effort, made off in all haste for Santa Maura, bearing with him the Standard of "the Religion" to be hung up in St. Sophia. The battle of Lepanto is fought and won: the Turks have been utterly vanquished.[1] Well might the good Pope cry, as the preacher cried in St. Stephen's a century later when Sobieski saved Vienna,[2] "*There was a man sent from* GOD, *whose name was* JOHN."

The Turkish fleet was almost annihilate: one hundred and ninety galleys were captured, besides galleots, and fifteen more burnt or sunk; probably twenty thousand men had perished, including an appalling list of high dignitaries from all parts of the empire. The Christians lost seven thousand five hundred men, including many of the most illustrious houses of Italy and Spain. Cervantes, who commanded a company of soldiers on board the *Marquesa*, fortunately escaped with a wound in his left arm; and to many the Battle of Lepanto is familiar only from the magical pages of *Don Quixote*. Seventeen

---

[1] Read the admirable and graphic description of the battle in JURIEN DE LA GRAVIÈRE, *La Guerre de Chypre et la Bataille de Lepante*, ii., 149-205.   [2] See the *Story of Turkey*, 237.

Venetian commanders were dead, and among them
Vicenzo Quirini and the valiant, chivalrous, and
venerable Proveditore Barbarigo. Sixty Knights of
the diminished Order of St. John had given up the
ghost. Twelve thousand Christian slaves were
freed from the Ottoman galleys.

The brilliant young conqueror did not wear his
well-earned laurels long. His statue was erected at
Messina ; his victory was the subject of Tintoret and
Titian ; he was received with ovations wherever he
went. Two years later he recaptured Tunis. Then
he was employed in the melancholy task of carrying
on Alva's detestable work in Flanders. He inflicted
a sanguinary defeat upon the Dutch at Gembloux,
and then, struck down by fever, the young hero died
on October 1, 1578, in his thirty-first year, the last
of the great figures of medieval chivalry—a knight
worthy to have been commemorated in the Charle-
magne *gestes* and to have sat at Arthur's Round
Table with Sir Galahad himself.

PART II.

THE PETTY PIRATES.

XV.

THE GENERAL OF THE GALLEYS.

16th, 17th, and 18th Centuries.

THE age of the great Corsairs may be said to have
ended with the battle of Lepanto, which sounded the
knell of the naval supremacy of the Ottomans. It
is true that they seemed to have lost little by Don
John's famous victory ; their beard was shorn, they
admitted, but it soon grew again :—their fleet was
speedily repaired, and the Venetians sued for peace.
But they had lost something more precious to them
than ships or men: their prestige was gone.
The powers of Christendom no longer dreaded to
meet the invincible Turk, for they had beaten him
once, and would beat him again. Rarely after this
did an Ottoman fleet sail proudly to work its
devastating way along the coasts of Italy. Small
raids there might be, but seldom a great adventure
such as Barbarossa or Sinān led. Crete might be
besieged for years ; but the Venetians, pressed by
land, nevertheless shattered the Turkish ships off
the coast. Damad 'Ali might recover the Morea, and
victoriously surround the shores of Greece with his
hundred sail ; but he would not venture to threaten

Venice, to lay siege to Nice, to harry Naples, or attack Malta. The Turks had enough to do to hold their own in the Black Sea against the encroaching forces of Russia.

Deprived of the protection which the prestige of the Turks had afforded, the Barbary Corsairs degenerated into petty pirates. They continued to waylay Christian cargoes, to ravish Christian villages, and carry off multitudes of captives ; but their depredations were not on the same grand scale, they robbed by stealth, and never invited a contest with ships of war. If caught, they would fight ; but their aim was plunder, and they had no fancy for broken bones gained out of mere ambition of conquest.

Ochiali was the last of the great Corsairs. He it was who, on his return to Constantinople after the fatal October 7, 1571, cheered the Sultan with the promise of revenge, was made Captain-Pasha, and sailed from the Bosphorus the following year with a fleet of two hundred and thirty vessels, just as though Lepanto had never been fought and lost. He sought for the Christian fleets, but could not induce them to offer battle. His operations in 1574 were limited to the recapture of Tunis, which Don John had restored to Spain in 1573. With two hundred and fifty galleys, ten *mahons* or galleasses, and thirty caramuzels, and supported by the Algerine squadron under Ahmed Pasha, Ochiali laid siege to the Goletta, which had owned a Spanish garrison ever since the conquest by Charles V. in 1535. Cervellon defended the fort till he had but a handful of men, and finally surrendered at discretion. Then Ochiali

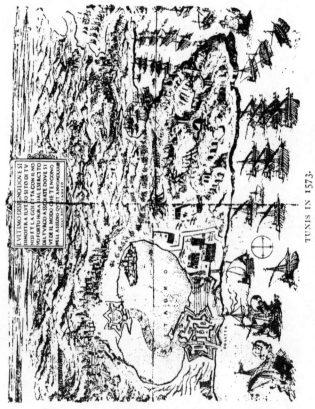

ULTIMO DISE-
DIMOSTRA IL VE
NISI ET LA GOL
VO FORTO HORA
DELTVRCO ASSE
VEDE IL MODO C
NELL ASEDIO QV

NO LOV E SI
RO SITO DI TV
ETTA CON IL NO
AL ESERCITO
DIATE DOVE SI
HE TENGONO

TUNIS IN 1573.

(From a Map in the British Museum.)

disappeared from the western seas ; he fought for his master in the Euxine during the Persian War, and died in 1580, aged seventy-two, with the reputation of the most powerful admiral that had ever held sway in the Golden Horn.

We have not closely followed the succession of the Pashas or Beglerbegs of Algiers, because more important affairs absorbed the whole energies of the Turkish galleys, and the rulers on land had little of consequence to do. Ochiali was the seventeenth pasha of Algiers, but of his predecessors, after the deaths of Urūj and Kheyr-ed-dīn Barbarossa, few attained special eminence. Hasan the son of Barbarossa took part in the siege of Malta, Sālih Reïs conquered Fez and Bujēya ; but the rest were chiefly occupied with repressing internal dissensions, fighting with their neighbours, and organizing small piratical expeditions. After Ochiali had been called to Stambol as Captain-Pasha, in 1572, when he had been Pasha of Algiers for four years, nine governors succeeded one another in twenty-four years. At first they were generally renegades : Ramadān the Sardinian (1574–7), Hasan the Venetian (1577–80 and 1582–3), Ja'far the Hungarian (1580–2), and Memi the Albanian (1583–6), followed one another, and (with the exception of the Venetian) proved to be wise, just, and clement rulers. Then the too usual practice was adopted of allotting the province to the highest bidder, and rich but incompetent or rascally Turks bought the reversion of the Pashalik. The reign of the renegades was over ; the Turks kept the government in their own hands, and the *rôle* of the ex-Christian adventurers was confined to the minor but more enterprising duties of a Corsair reïs or the "general of the galleys." The Pashas, and afterwards the Deys, with occasional exceptions, gave up commanding piratical expeditions, and the interest of the history now turns upon the captains of galleys.

Piracy without and bloodshed and anarchy within form the staple of the records. Tunis, Tripoli, and Algiers showed very similar symptoms. Tripoli was the least powerful, and therefore the least injurious ; Algiers dominated the Western Mediterranean and to a considerable extent the Atlantic ; Tunis, less venturesome, but still formidable, infested the Eastern Mediterranean, and made the passage of Malta and the Adriatic its special hunting grounds. At Tunis thirty Deys, appointed by the Sublime Porte, succeeded one another from 1590 to 1705—giving each an average reign of less than four years. Most of them were deposed, many murdered, and one is related on credible authority to have been torn to pieces and devoured by the enraged populace. In 1705 the soldiery, following the example of Algiers, elected their own governor, and called him Bey ; and the Porte was obliged to acquiesce. Eleven Beys followed one another, up to the French "protectorate." The external history of these three centuries is made up of lawless piracy and the levying of blackmail from most of the trading powers of Europe, accompanied by acts of insufferable insolence towards the foreign representatives ; all of which was accepted submissively by kings and governments, insomuch that William III. treated a flagrant Corsair, 'Ali Reïs, who had become Dey, with the courtesy due to a monarch, and signed himself his "loving friend." The earliest English treaty with Tunis was dated 1662; many more followed, and all were about equally inefficacious. Civil anarchy, quarrels with France, and wars with Algiers, generally stopped "by order" of the helpless Porte, fill up the details of this uninteresting canvas.

Precisely the same picture is afforded by the modern annals of Algiers. Take the Deys at the beginning of the eighteenth century. Hasan Chāwush was deposed in 1700, and succeeded by the Aga of the Sipāhis, Mustafa, nicknamed *Bogotillos* or "Whiskerandos," who, though something of a coward, engaged in two successful campaigns against Tunis and one with Morocco, until he had the misfortune to find the bow-string round his throat in 1706. Uzeyn Khōja followed, and Oran fell during his one year's reign, after which he was banished to the mountains, and died. Bektāsh Khōja, the next Dey, was murdered on his judgment-seat in the third year of his reign. A fifth Dey, Ibrahīm Deli, or "the Fool," made himself so hated by his unconscionable licentiousness that he was assassinated, and his mutilated body exposed in the street, within a few months, and 'Ali, who succeeded in 1710, by murdering some three thousand Turks, contrived to reign eight years, and by some mistake died in his bed.

The kingdom of Morocco is not strictly a Barbary state, and its history does not belong to this volume

Nevertheless, the operations of the Morocco pirates outside the Straits of Gibraltar so closely resemble those of the Algerine Corsairs within, that a few words about them will not be out of place. At one time Tetwān, within the Straits, in spite of its exposed haven, was a famous place for rovers, but its prosperity was destroyed by Philip II. in 1564. Ceuta was always semi-European, half Genoese, then Portuguese(1415), and finally Spanish(1570 to this day). Tangiers, as the dowry of Charles II.'s Queen, Catherine of Portugal, was for some time English territory. Spanish forts at Peñon de Velez de la Gomera and Alhucemas, and Portuguese garrisons, repressed piracy in their vicinity ; and in later times Salē was perhaps the only port in Morocco that sent forth buccaneers. Reefs of rocks and drifts of sand render the west coast unsuitable for anchorage, and the roads are unsafe when the wind is in the south-west. Consequently the piracy of Salē, though notorious and dreaded by merchantmen, was on a small scale ; large vessels could not enter the harbour, and two-hundred-ton ships had to be lightened before they could pass the bar. The cruisers of Salē were therefore built very light and small, with which they did not dare to attack considerable and well-armed ships. Indeed, Capt. Delgarno and his twenty-gun frigate so terrified the Salē rovers, that they never ventured forth while he was about, and mothers used to quiet naughty children by saying that Delgarno was coming for them, just as Napoleon and " Malbrouk " were used as bugbears in England and France. There was not a single full-sized galley at Salē in

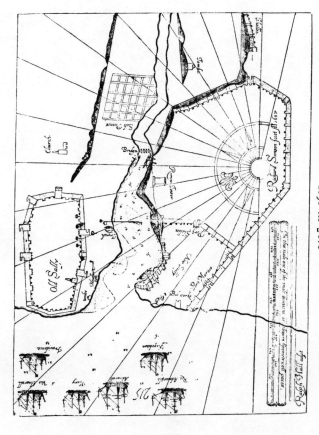

SALE IN 1637.

(From a Map in the British Museum.)

1634, and accounts a hundred years later agree that
the Salē rovers had but insignificant vessels, and very
few of them, while their docks were practically dis-
used, in spite of abundance of timber. In the latter
part of the eighteenth century there seems to have
been an increase in the depredations of the Salē
pirates, which probably earned them their exag-
gerated reputation. At that time they had vessels
of thirty and thirty-six guns, but unwieldy and
badly built, with which they captured Provençal
ships and did considerable mischief, till the Chevalier
Acton in 1773, with a single Tuscan frigate, destroyed
three out of their five ships. About 1788 the whole
Morocco navy consisted of six or eight frigates of
two hundred tons, armed with fourteen to eighteen
six-pounders, and some galleys. The rovers of Salē
formed at one time a sort of republic of pirates,
paying the emperor a tithe of prize-money and
slaves, in return for non-interference ; but gradually
the Government absorbed most of the profits, and the
trade declined, till the emperors, in return for rich
presents, concluded treaties with the chief maritime
Powers, and to a large extent suppressed piracy.[1]

Turning from the monotonous records of internal

---

[1] See JOHN WINDUS, *Journey to Mequinez* (Lond., 1735), describing
the embassy of Commodore Stewart to Morocco, in 1721, when two
hundred and ninety-six English slaves were freed, and a treaty repudiating piracy and the right of search was concluded. Capt. JOHN
BRAITHWAITE'S *History of the Revolutions in Morocco* (1729) includes
a journal of events and observations made during Mr. Russell's mission
in 1728. Salē is described at pp. 343 ff. See also CHENIER, *Present
State of the Empire of Morocco* (Eng. transl., 1788). Chenier was
French Consul from 1767 : the original work is entitled *Recherches
historiques sur les Maures.*

barbarism, the more adventurous side of Algerine
history claims a brief notice. Among the captains
who continued to make the name of Corsair terrible
to Christian ears, Murād Reïs holds the foremost
place ; indeed, he belongs to the order of great
Corsairs. There were several of the name, and this
Murād was distinguished as the Great Murād. He
was an Arnaut or Albanian, who was captured by an
Algerine pirate at the age of twelve, and early
showed a turn for adventure. When his patron was
engaged at the siege of Malta in 1565, young Murād
gave him the slip, and went on a private cruise of his
own, in which he contrived to split his galleot upon a
rock. Undeterred by this misadventure, as soon as
he got back to Algiers he set out in a brigantine of
fifteen banks, and speedily brought back three
Spanish prizes and one hundred and forty Christians.
He was with Ochiali when that eminent rover seized
Saint-Clément's galleys, and was with difficulty
restrained from anticipating his admiral in boarding
the *St. Ann.* He soon gained the reputation
of a Corsair of the first water, and " a person,
who, for our sins, did more harm to the Christians
than any other." In 1578, while cruising about the
Calabrian coast with eight galleots in search of prey,
he sighted the *Capitana* of Sicily and a consort, with
the Duke of Tierra Nuova and his retinue on board.
After a hot pursuit the consort was caught at sea ;
the flagship ran on shore ; the Duke and all the
ship's company deserted her ; and the beautiful vessel
was safely brought into Algiers harbour. In 1585
Murād ventured out into the Atlantic out of sight

of land, which no Algerine had ever dared to do
before, and picking up a reinforcement of small
brigantines at Salē, descended at daybreak upon
Lanzarote, one of the Canary Islands, sacked the
town without opposition, and carried off the governor's
family and three hundred captives. This done, he
unblushingly ran up a flag of truce, and permitted
the Count and the chief families to come on board
and buy back their relations. In 1589, after picking
up a stray trader or two, he fell in with *La Serena*,
a galley of Malta, which had a Turkish prize in tow.
Far from shirking a conflict with so formidable an
antagonist, Murād gave hot pursuit with his single
galleot, and coming up with the *Serena*, boarded and
mastered her in half an hour. Then, after stopping
to arrest the misdoings of a Majorcan pirate, who was
poaching on his own private manor, the Corsair
carried his prizes into Algiers, where he was honour-
ably mounted on the Pasha's own horse and escorted
in triumph to the Palace by a guard of Janissaries.
In 1594, when he had attained the dignity of
" General of the Algerine Galleys," Murād, with four
galleots, encountered two Tuscan galleys off Tripoli ;
lowering the masts of two of his galleots, so that
they should escape observation, he towed them
behind the other two, and when the Tuscans had
drawn near in full expectation of a couple of prizes,
he loosed the vessels astern, and with all four bore
down upon the enemy ; both galleys were taken, and
the Florentine knights and soldiers were chained to the
oars in place of the Turks who had lately sat there.[1]

[1] MORGAN, 557–9, 588, 597, 607.

14

No more typical example of the later sort of pirate
can be cited than 'Ali Pichinin, General of the Galleys
and galleons of Algiers in the middle of the seventeenth century.   This notable slaver, without Barbarossa's ambition or nobility, possessed much of his
daring and seamanship.   In 1638, emboldened by
the successes of the Sultan Murād IV. against the
Persians, 'Ali put to sea, and, picking up some
Tunisian galleys at Bizerta, set sail with a squadron
of sixteen for the east coast of Italy.   He sacked
the district of Nicotra in Apulia, carrying off great
spoils and many captives, not sparing even nuns ;
and then scoured the Adriatic, took a ship in sight
of Cattaro, and picked up every stray vessel that
could be found.

Upon this a strong Venetian squadron, under
Marino Capello, sallied forth, and compelled the
Corsairs to seek shelter under the guns of the
Turkish fortress of Valona in Albania.   In spite of
the peace then subsisting between Venice and the
Porte, Capello attacked, and the fortress naturally
defended, the refugees.   The Corsairs were obliged
to land, and then Capello, carried away by his zeal,
and in contravention of his orders, sent in his galleots
and, after a sharp struggle, towed away the whole
Barbary squadron, leaving 'Ali and his unlucky
followers amazed upon the beach.   For this bold
stroke Capello was severely reprimanded by the
Senate, and the Porte was consoled for the breach of
treaty by a *douceur* of five hundred thousand ducats :
but meanwhile the better part of the Algerine galley-
fleet had ceased to exist, and owners and captains

were bankrupt. It was small consolation that in the same summer an expedition to the north, piloted by a renegade from Iceland, brought back eight hundred of his unfortunate countrymen to exchange the cold of their native land for the bagnios of Algiers.

In 1641, however, the Corsairs had recovered from their losses, and 'Ali Pichinin could boast a fleet of at least sixty-five vessels, as we have it on the authority of Emanuel d'Aranda, who was his slave at the time. The wealth and power of the General of the Galleys were then at their zenith. Six hundred slaves were nightly locked up in his prison, which afterwards was known as the Khan of 'Ali Pichinin, and in Morgan's time was noted for its grape vines, which covered the walls and fringed the windows with the luscious fruit up to the top storey. The son of a renegade himself, he liked not that his followers should turn Turk upon his hands; which " was but picking his pocket of so much money to give a disciple to Mohammed, for whom he was remarked to have no extraordinary veneration. He had actually cudgelled a Frenchmen out of the name of Mustafa (which he had assumed with a Turkish dress) into that of John, which he would fain have renounced. His farms and garden-houses were also under the directions of his own Christians. I have heard much discourse of an entertainment he once made, at his garden, for all the chief Armadores and Corsairs, at which the Pasha was also a guest, but found his own victuals, as fearing some foul play; nothing of which is ill taken among the Turks. All was dressed at town in the general's own kitchen, and passed along

from hand to hand by his slaves up to the garden-
house, above two miles' distant, where as much of the
victuals as got safe thither arrived smoking hot, as
they tell the story." [1] A good part, however, disappeared on the road, since, in Corsair's phrase, "the
Christian slaves wore hooks on their fingers," and
the guests went nigh to be starved. 'Ali's plan for
feeding his slaves was characteristic. He gave them
no loaves as others did, but told them they were
indeed a sorry set of scoundrels, unworthy of the
name of slaves, if, during the two or three hours of
liberty they enjoyed before sunset, they could not
find enough to keep them for a day. His bagnios
used to be regular auction-rooms for stolen goods,
and were besieged by indignant victims, who were
reproached for their carelessness, and made to re-
purchase their own valuables : in fine, 'Ali Pichinin
"has the honour of having trained up the cleanest
set of thieves that were anywhere to be met with."
Once a slave found a costly ring of the general's, and
restored to him without price : for which "unseason-
able piece of honesty" 'Ali gave him half a ducat,
and called him a fool for his pains ; the ring was
worth his ransom. Another time, a slave bargained
to sell to an ironmaster the general's anchor from out
of his own galley : when discovered, he was commended for his enterprising spirit, and told he was
fit to be a slave, since he knew how to gain his living.
This slave-dealer had a genius for wheedling the truth
out of captives ; he was so civil and sympathizing
when a new prize was caught, so ready with his

[1] MORGAN, 674.

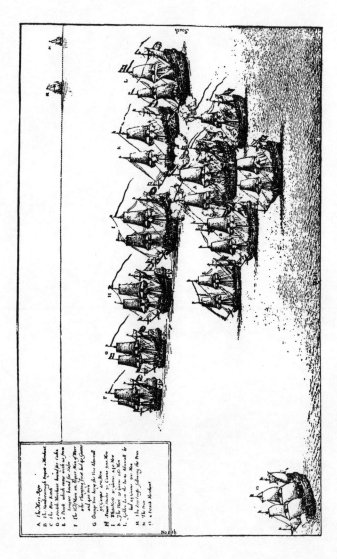

FIGHT OF THE "MARY ROSE" WITH ALGERINE PIRATES, 1669.

(*Ogilby's Africa*, 1670.)

"Count" and "my lord" to plain gentlemen, and his "your Eminence" to simple clergymen, that they soon confided in him, revealed their rank, and had their ransom fixed : but, to do him justice, he kept his word, and once promised the release was certain : "My word is my word," he would say.

He was a man of very free views in religion. Once he asked a Genoese priest to tell him candidly what would become of him ; "frankly," said Father Angelo, "I am persuaded that the devil will have you ; " and the response was cheerfully accepted. Another time it was a devout Moslem sheykh who begged 'Ali to give him a Christian slave to kill, as he did not feel that he had offered any sufficiently pleasing sacrifice to the prophet Mohammed. 'Ali unchained the stroke-oar of his galley, a muscular Spaniard, and armed him at all points, and sent him to be killed by the holy man. "This Christian," shrieked the good sheykh, running as hard as he could, "looks as if he rather wanted to kill me than to be killed himself." "So is it," said Ali, "that you are to merit the prophet's favour. Thus it is that Christians are to be sacrificed. Mohammed was a brave, generous man, and never thought it any service done him to slaughter those who were not able to defend themselves. Go ; get yourself better instructed in the meaning of the Koran." He was a thorough Corsair, with the rough code of honour, as well as the unprincipled rascality of the sea-rover.

XVI.

16th Century.

" THE Corsairs," says Haedo, " are those who support themselves by continual sea-robberies; and,
admitting that among their numbers some of them
are natural Turks, Moors, &c, yet the main body of
them are renegadoes from every part of Christendom;
all who are extremely well acquainted with the
Christian coasts." It is a singular fact that the
majority of these plunderers of Christians were themselves born in the Faith. In the long list of Algerine
viceroys, we meet with many a European. Barbarossa himself was born in Lesbos, probably of a
Greek mother. His successor was a Sardinian; soon
afterwards a Corsican became pasha of Algiers, then
another Sardinian; Ochiali was a Calabrian; Ramadān came from Sardinia, and was succeeded by a
Venetian, who in turn gave place to a Hungarian,
who made room for an Albanian. In 1588 the thirty-
five galleys or galleots of Algiers were commanded
by eleven Turks and twenty-four renegades, including nations of France, Venice, Genoa, Sicily,

Naples, Spain, Greece, Calabria, Corsica, Albania, and Hungary, and a Jew. In short, up to nearly the close of the sixteenth century (but much more rarely afterwards) the chiefs of the Corsairs and the governors were commonly drawn from Christian lands. Some of them volunteered—and to the outlaws of Europe the command of a Barbary galley was perhaps the only congenial resort ;—but most of them were captives seized as children, and torn from their homes in some of the Corsairs' annual raids upon Corsica and Sardinia and the Italian or Dalmatian coasts. Most of such prisoners were condemned to menial and other labour, unless ransomed ; but the bolder and handsomer boys were often picked out by the penetrating eye of the reïs, and once chosen the young captive's career was established.

"While the Christians with their galleys are at repose, sounding their trumpets in the harbours, and very much at their ease regaling themselves, passing the day and night in banqueting, cards, and dice, the Corsairs at pleasure are traversing the east and west seas, without the least fear or apprehension, as free and absolute sovereigns thereof. Nay, they roam them up and down no otherwise than do such as go in chase of hares for their diversion. They here snap up a ship laden with gold and silver from India, and there another richly fraught from Flanders ; now they make prize of a vessel from England, then of another from Portugal. Here they board and lead away one ʿrom Venice, then one from Sicily, and a little further on they swoop down upon others from Naples, Livorno, or Genoa, all of them abundantly crammed with great and wonderful riches. And at other times carrying with them as guides renegadoes (of which there are in Algiers vast numbers of all Christian nations, nay, the generality of the Corsairs are no other than renegadoes, and all of them exceedingly well acquainted with the coasts of Christendom, and even within the land), they very deliberately, even at noon-day, or indeed just when they please, leap ashore, and walk on without the least dread, and advance into the country, ten, twelve, or fifteen leagues or more ; and the poor Christians, thinking themselves secure, are surprised unawares ; many towns, villages, and farms sacked ; and infinite numbers of souls, men, women, children, and infants at the breast, dragged away into a wretched captivity. With these miserable ruined people, loaded with their own valuable substance, they retreat leisurely, with eyes full of laughter and content, to their vessels. In this manner, as is too well known, they have utterly ruined and destroyed Sardinia, Corsica, Sicily, Calabria, the neighbourhoods of Naples, Rome, and Genoa, all the Balearic islands, and the whole coast of Spain : in which last more particularly they feast it as they think fit, on account of the Moriscos who inhabit there ; who being all more zealous Mohammedans than are the very Moors born in Barbary, they receive and caress the Corsairs, and give them notice of whatever they desire to be informed of. Insomuch that before these Corsairs have been absent from their abodes much longer than perhaps twenty or thirty days, they return home rich, with their vessels crowded with captives, and ready to sink with

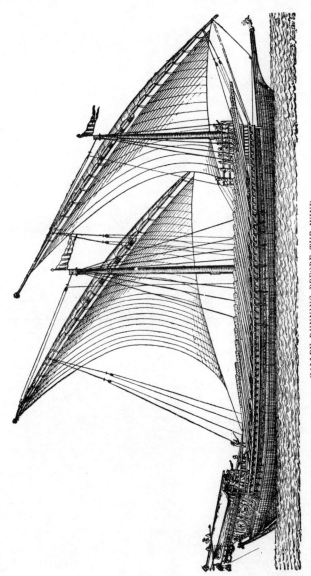

GALLEY RUNNING BEFORE THE WIND.

(*Jurien de la Gravière.*)

wealth ; in one instant, and with scarce any trouble, reaping the fruits of all that the avaricious Mexican and greedy Peruvian have been digging from the bowels of the earth with such toil and sweat, and the thirsty merchant with such manifest perils has for so long been scraping together, and has been so many thousand leagues to fetch away, either from the east or west, with inexpressible danger and fatigue. Thus they have crammed most of the houses, the magazines, and all the shops of this Den of Thieves with gold, silver, pearls, amber, spices, drugs, silks, cloths, velvets, &c., whereby they have rendered this city the most opulent in the world : insomuch that the Turks call it, not without reason, their India, their Mexico, their Peru." [1]

One has some trouble in realizing the sort of navigation employed by Corsairs. We must disabuse our minds of all ideas of tall masts straining under a weight of canvas, sail above sail. The Corsairs' vessels were long narrow row-boats, carrying indeed a sail or two, but depending for safety and movement mainly upon the oars. The boats were called galleys, galleots, brigantines ("*galeotas ligeras o vergātines*," or *frigatas*), &c., according to their size : a galleot is a small galley, while a brigantine may be called a quarter galley. The number of men to each oar varies, too, according to the vessel's size : a galley may have as many as four to six men working side by side to each oar, a galleot but two or three, and a brigantine one ; but in so small a craft as the last each man must be a fighter as well as an oarsmen, whereas the

---

[1] HAEDO, quoted by MORGAN, 593-4.

larger vessels of the Corsairs were rowed entirely by Christian slaves.

The galley is the type of all these vessels, and those who are curious about the minutest details of building and equipping galleys need only consult Master Joseph Furttenbach's *Architectura Navalis : Das ist, Von dem Schiff-Gebaw, auf dem Meer und Seekusten zu gebrauchen,*" printed in the town of Ulm, in the Holy Roman Empire, by Jonam Saurn, in 1629. Any one could construct a galley from the numerous plans and elevations and sections and finished views (some of which are here reproduced) in this interesting and precise work.[1] Furttenbach is an enthusiastic admirer of a ship's beauties, and he had seen all varieties ; for his trade took him to Venice, where he had a galleasse,[2] and he had doubtless viewed many

---

[1] Hardly less valuable is Adm. JURIEN DE LA GRAVIÈRE'S *Les Derniers Jours de la Marine à Rames* (Paris, 1885). It contains an admirable account of the French galley system, the mode of recruiting, discipline, and general management ; a description of the different classes of vessels, and their manner of navigation ; while a learned Appendix of over one hundred pages describes the details of galley-building, finishing, fitting, and rigging, and everything that the student need wish to learn. The chapters (ix. and x.) on *Navigation à la rame* and *Navigation à la voile,* are particularly worth reading by those who would understand sixteenth and seventeenth century seamanship.

[2] A galleasse was originally a large heavy galley, three-masted, and fitted with a rudder, since its bulk compelled it to trust to sails as well as oars. It was a sort of transition-ship, between the galley and the galleon, and as time went on it became more and more of a sailing ship. It had high bulwarks, with loopholes for muskets, and there was at least a partial cover for the crew. The Portuguese galleys in the Spanish Armada mounted each 110 soldiers and 222 galley-slaves ; but the Neapolitan galleasses carried 700 men, of whom 130 were sailors, 270 soldiers, and 300 slaves of the oar. JURIEN DE LA GRAVIÈRE, *Les Derniers Jours de la Marine à Rames,* 65–7.

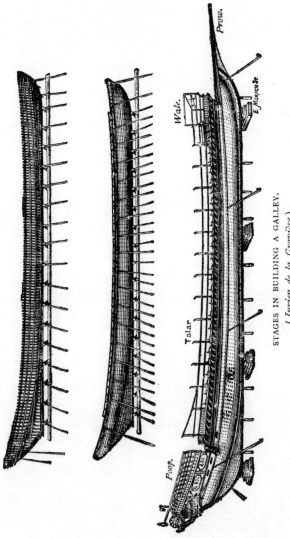

STAGES IN BUILDING A GALLEY.

(*Jurien de la Gravière.*)

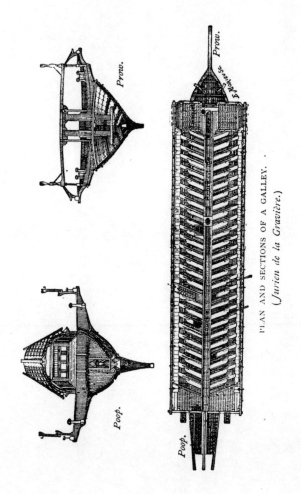

PLAN AND SECTIONS OF A GALLEY.
(*Jurien de la Gravière.*)

Prow.

Prow.

Poop.

Poop.

15

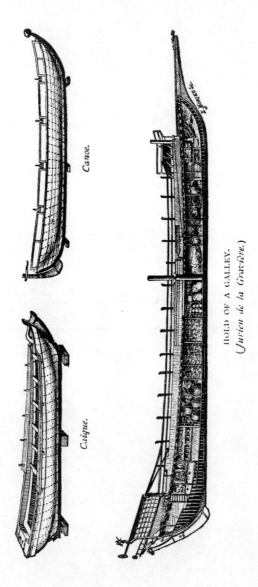

Canoe.

Cuique.

HOLD OF A GALLEY.
(*Jurien de la Gravière.*)

a Corsair fleet, since he could remember the battle of Lepanto and the death of Ochiali. His zeal runs clean away with him when he describes a *stolo*, or great flagship (*capitanea galea*) of Malta in her pomp and dignity and lordliness, as she rides the seas to the rhythmical beat of her many oars, or " easies " with every blade suspended motionless above the waves like the wings of a poised falcon. A galley such as this is " a princely, nay, a royal and imperial *vassello di remo*," and much the most suitable, he adds, for the uses of peace and of war in the Mediterranean Sea. A galley may be 180 or 190 spans long—Furttenbach measures a ship by *palmi*, which varied from nine to ten inches in different places in Italy,—say 150 feet, the length of an old seventy-four frigate, but with hardly a fifth of its cubit contents—and its greatest beam is 25 spans broad. The one engraved on p. 37 is evidently an admiral's galley of the Knights of Malta. She carries two masts—the *albero maestro* or mainmast, and the *trinchetto*, or foremast, each with a great lateen sail. The Genoese and Venetians set the models of these vessels, and the Italian terms were generally used in all European navigation till the northern nations took the lead in sailing ships. These sails are often clewed up, however, for the mariner of the sixteenth century was ill-practised in the art of tacking, and very fearful of losing sight of land for long, so that unless he had a wind fair astern he preferred to trust to his oars. A short deck at the prow and poop serve, the one to carry the fighting-men and trumpeters and yardsmen, and to provide cover for the four guns, the other to accommodate the knights and gentlemen, and especially the admiral or captain, who sits at the stern under a red damask canopy embroidered with gold, surveying the crew, surrounded by the chivalry of " the Religion," whose white cross waves on the taffety standard over their head, and shines upon various pennants and burgees aloft. Behind, overlooking the roof of the poop, stands the pilot who steers the ship by the tiller in his hand.

Between the two decks, in the ship's waist, is the propelling power : fifty-four benches or banks, twenty-seven a side, support each four or five slaves, whose whole business in life is to tug at the fifty-four oars. This flagship is a Christian vessel, so the rowers are either Turkish and Moorish captives, or Christian convicts. If it were a Corsair, the rowers would all be Christian prisoners. In earlier days the galleys were rowed by freemen, and so late as 1500 the Moors of Algiers pulled their own brigantines to the attack of Spanish villages, but their boats were light, and a single man could pull the oar. Two or three were needed for a galleot, and as many sometimes as six for each oar of a large galley. It was impossible to induce freemen to toil at the oar, sweating close together, for hour after hour—not sitting, but leaping on the bench, in order to throw their whole weight on the oar. " Think of six men chained to a bench, naked as when they were born, one foot on the stretcher, the other on the bench in front, holding an immensely heavy oar [fifteen feet long], bending forwards to the stern with arms at full reach to clear the backs of the rowers in front, who bend likewise ; and then having got forward, shoving up the oar's end to let the blade catch the water, then throwing their bodies back on to the groaning bench. A galley oar sometimes pulls thus for ten, twelve, or even twenty hours without a moment's rest. The boatswain, or other sailor, in such a stress, puts a piece of bread steeped in wine in the wretched rower's mouth to stop fainting, and then the captain shouts the order to redouble the lash. If a slave falls exhausted upon his oar (which often chances) he is flogged till he is taken for dead, and then pitched unceremoniously into the sea." [1]

"Those who have not seen a galley at sea, especially in chasing or being chased, cannot well conceive the shock such a spectacle must give to a heart capable of the least tincture of commiseration. To behold ranks and files of half-naked, half-starved, half-tanned meagre wretches, chained to a plank, from whence they remove not for months together (commonly half a year), urged on, even beyond human strength, with cruel and repeated blows on their bare flesh, to an incessant continuation of the most violent of all exercises ; and this for whole days and nights successively, which often happens in a furious chase, when one party, like vultures, is hurried on almost as eagerly after their prey, as is the weaker party hurried away in hopes of preserving life and liberty." [2]

Sometimes a galley-slave worked as long as twenty years, sometimes for all his miserable life, at this

---

[1] So says Jean Marteille de Bergerac, a galley-slave about 1701, quoted by Adm. JURIEN DE LA GRAVIÈRE, *Derniers Jours de la Marine à Rames*, 13.   [2] MORGAN, 517.

fearful calling. The poor creatures were chained so
close together in their narrow bench—a sharp cut was
the characteristic of the galley—that they could not
sleep at full length. Sometimes seven men (on French
galleys, too, in the last century), had to live and sleep
in a space ten feet by four. The whole ship was a
sea of hopeless faces. And between the two lines of
rowers ran the bridge, and on it stood two boatswains
(*comiti*) armed with long whips, which they laid on to
the bare backs of the rowers with merciless severity.
Furttenbach gives a picture of the two boatswains
in grimly humorous verse : how they stand,

> Beclad, belaced, betrimmed, with many knots bespick ;
> Embroidered, padded, tied ; all feathers and all flap ;
> Curly and queued, equipped, curious of hood and cap :

and how they "ever stolidly smite" the crew with the
bastinado,

> Or give them a backward prod in the naked flesh as they ply,
> With the point that pricks like a goad, when "powder and shot" is
>   the cry ;

in order to send the Turks to Davy's wet locker :—

> As John of Austria nipped them and riddled them with ball,
> As soon as his eyes fell on them, and ducked or slaughtered them all ;

and how the boatswain's dreaded whistle shrieked
through the ship :—

> For they hearken to such a blast through all the swish and sweat,
> Through rattle and rumpus and raps, and the kicks and cuffs that they
>   get,
> Through the chatter and tread, and the rudder's wash, and the dismal
>   clank
> Of the shameful chain which forever binds the slave to the bank.

To this may be added Captain Pantero Pantera's description of the boatswain's demeanour : "He should appear kindly towards the crew : assist it, pet it, but without undue familiarity ; be, in short, its guardian and in some sort its father, remembering that, when all's said, 'tis human flesh, and human flesh in direst misery."

This terrible living grave of a galley, let us remember, is depicted from Christian models. A hundred and fifty years ago such scenes might be witnessed on many a European vessel. The Corsairs of Algiers only served their enemies as they served them : their galley slaves were no worse treated, to say the least, than were Doria's or the King of France's own. Rank and delicate nurture were respected on neither side : a gallant Corsair like Dragut had to drag his chain and pull his insatiable oar like any convict at the treadmill, and a future grand master of Malta might chance to take his seat on the rowing bench beside commonest scoundrel of Naples. No one seemed to observe the horrible brutality of the service, where each man, let him be never so refined, was compelled to endure the filth and vermin of his neighbour who might be half a savage and was bound to become wholly one ; and when Madame de Grignan wrote an account of a visit to a galley, her friend Madame de Sévigné replied that she would "much like to see this sort of Hell," and the men "groaning day and night under the weight of their chains." *Autres temps, autres moeurs !*

Furttenbach tells us much more about the galley ; and how it was rigged out with brilliant cloths on the bulwarks on fête-days ; how the biscuit was made to

last six or eight months, each slave getting twenty-
eight ounces thrice a week, and a spoonful of some
mess of rice or bones or green stuff ; of the trouble
of keeping the water-cans under the benches full and
fairly fresh.   The full complement of a large galley
included, he says, besides about 270 rowers, and the
captain, chaplain, doctor, scrivener, boatswains, and
master, or pilot, ten or fifteen gentleman adventurers,
friends of the captain, sharing his mess, and berthed
in the poop ; twelve helmsmen (*timonieri*), six foretop
A.B's., ten warders for the captives, twelve ordinary
seamen, four gunners, a carpenter, smith, cooper, and a
couple of cooks, together with fifty or sixty soldiers ;
so that the whole equipage of a fighting-galley must
have reached a total of about four hundred men.[1]

What is true of a European galley is also generally
applicable to a Barbary galleot, except that the latter
was generally smaller and lighter, and had commonly
but one mast, and no castle on the prow.[2]   The
Algerines preferred fighting on galleots of eighteen to
twenty-four banks of oars, as more manageable than
larger ships.   The crew of about two hundred men
was very densely packed, and about one hundred
soldiers armed with muskets, bows, and scimitars
occupied the poop.   Haedo has described the general
system of the Corsairs as he knew it at the close of the
sixteenth century, and his account, here summarized,
holds good for earlier and somewhat later periods :—

---

[1] In 1630 a French galley's company consisted of 250 forçats and 116
officers, soldiers, and sailors.

[2] DAN, *Hist. de Barbarie*, 268–71.   See the cut of Tunisian galleots
on p. 183.

These vessels are perpetually building or repairing at Algiers ; the builders are all Christians, who have a monthly pay from the Treasury of six, eight, or ten quarter-dollars, with a daily allowance of three loaves of the same bread with the Turkish soldiery, who have four. Some of the upper rank of these masters have six and even eight of these loaves ; nor has any of their workmen, as carpenters, caulkers, coopers, oar-makers, smiths, &c., fewer than three. The *Beylik*, or common magazine, never wants slaves of all useful callings, " nor is it probable that they should ever have a scarcity of such while they are continually bringing in incredible numbers of Christians of all nations." The captains, too, have their private artificer slaves, whom they buy for high prices and take with them on the cruise, and hire them out to help the Beylik workmen when ashore.

The number of vessels possessed at any one time by the Algerines appears to have never been large. Barbarossa and Dragut were content with small squadrons. Ochiali had but fifteen Algerine galleys at Lepanto. Haedo says that at the close of the sixteenth century (1581) the Algerines possessed 36 galleots or galleys, made up of 3 of 24 banks, 1 of 23, 11 of 22, 8 of 20, 1 of 19, 10 of 18, and 2 of 15, and these were, all but 14, commanded by renegades. They had besides a certain number of brigantines of 14 banks, chiefly belonging to Moors at Shershēl. This agrees substantially with Father Dan's account (1634), who says that there were in 1588 thirty-five galleys or brigantines (he means galleots) of which all but eleven were commanded by renegades. Haedo gives the

list [1] of the 35 captains, from which the following
names are selected: Ja'far the Pasha (Hungarian),
Memi (Albanian), Murād (French), Deli Memi
(Greek), Murād Reïs (Albanian), Feru Reïs (Genoese),
Murād Maltrapillo and Yūsuf (Spaniards), Memi Reïs
and Memi Gancho (Venetians), Murād the Less
(Greek), Memi the Corsican, Memi the Calabrian,
Montez the Sicilian, and so forth, most of whom com-
manded galleys of 22 to 24 banks.[2]

It was a pretty sight to see the launching of a
galley. After the long months of labour, after felling
the oak and pine in the forests of Shershēl, and carrying the fashioned planks on camels, mules, or their
own shoulders, some thirty miles to the seashore; or
perhaps breaking up some unwieldy prize vessel taken
from the Spaniards or Venetians; after all the sawing
and fitting and caulking and painting; then at last
comes the day of rejoicing for the Christian slaves who
alone have done the work: for no Mussulman would
offer to put a finger to the building of a vessel, saving
a few Morisco oar-makers and caulkers. Then the
armadores, or owners of the new galleot, as soon as it is
finished, come down with presents of money and clothes,
and hang them upon the mast and rigging, to the value
of two hundred or three hundred ducats, to be divided
among their slaves, whose only pay till that day has
been the daily loaves. Then again on the day of
launching, after the vessel has been keeled over, and
the bottom carefully greased from stem to stern, more
presents from owners and captains to the workmen,
to say nothing of a hearty dinner; and a great

---

[1] *Topographia*, 18.   [2] DAN, 270-1.

straining and shoving of brawny arms and bare backs, a shout of *Allahu Akbar*, " God is Most Great," as the sheep is slaughtered over the vessel's prow—a symbol, they said, of the Christian blood to be shed—and the galleot glides into the water prepared for her career of devastation : built by Christians and manned by Christians, commanded probably by a quondam Christian, she sallies forth to prey upon Christendom.

The rowers, if possible, were all Christian slaves, belonging to the owners, but when these were not numerous enough, other slaves, or Arabs and Moors, were hired at ten ducats the trip, prize or no prize. If he was able, the captain (*Reïs*) would build and furnish out his own vessel, entirely at his own cost, in hope of greater profit ; but often he had not the means, and then he would call in the aid of one or more *armadores*. These were often speculative shop-keepers, who invested in a part share of a galleot on the chance of a prize, and who often discovered that ruin lay in so hazardous a lottery. The complement of soldiers, whether volunteers (*levents*), consisting of Turks, renegades, or *Kuroghler* (*Kuloghler*)—*i.e.*, *creoles*, natives, Turks born on the soil—or if these cannot be had, ordinary Moors, or Ottoman janis-saries, varied with the vessel's size, but generally was calculated at two to each oar, because there was just room for two men to sit beside each bank of rowers : they were not paid unless they took a prize, nor were they supplied with anything more than biscuit, vinegar, and oil—everything else, even their blankets, they found themselves. The soldiers were under the command of their own Aga, who was entirely in-

dependent of the Reïs and formed an efficient check
upon that officer's conduct. Vinegar and water, with
a few drops of oil on the surface, formed the chief
drink of the galley slaves, and their food was
moistened biscuit or rusk, and an occasional mess of
gruel (*burgol*) : nor was this given out when hard
rowing was needed, for oars move slackly on a full
stomach.

It was usual to consult an auguration book and
a *marabut*, or saint, before deciding on a fortunate
day for putting to sea, and these saints expected
a share of the prize money. Fridays and Sundays
were the favourite days for sailing ; a gun is fired
in honour of their tutelary patron ; "God speed
us!" shout the crew ; "God send you a prize!"
reply the crowd on the shore, and the galleot swiftly
glides away on its destructive path. "The Algerines,"
says Haedo, "generally speaking, are out upon the
cruise winter and summer, the whole year round ; and
so devoid of dread they roam these eastern and
western seas, laughing all the while at the Christian
galleys (which lie trumpetting, gaming, and banqueting in the ports of Christendom), neither more nor
less than if they went a hunting hares and rabbits,
killing here one and there another. Nay, far from
being under apprehension, they are certain of their
game ; since their galleots are so extremely light and
nimble, and in such excellent order, as they always
are [1] ; whereas, on the contrary, the Christian galleys

---

[1] The Corsairs prided themselves on the ship-shape appearance of
their vessels. Everything was stowed away with marvellous neatness
and economy of space and speed ; even the anchor was lowered into

are so heavy, so embarrassed, and in such bad order
and confusion, that it is utterly in vain to think of
giving them chase, or of preventing them from going
and coming, and doing just as they their selves
please. This is the occasion that, when at any time
the Christian galleys chase them, their custom is, by
way of game and sneer, to point to their fresh-
tallowed poops, as they glide along like fishes before
them, all one as if they showed them their backs to
salute : and as in the cruising art, by continual practise,
they are so very expert, and withal (for our sins) so
daring, presumptuous, and fortunate, in a few days
from their leaving Algiers they return laden with
infinite wealth and captives ; and are able to make
three or four voyages in a year, and even more if they
are inclined to exert themselves. Those who have
been cruising westward, when they have taken a prize,
conduct it to sell at Tetwān, El-Araish, &c., in the
kingdom of Fez ; as do those who have been eastward, in the states of Tunis and Tripoli : where,
refurnishing themselves with provisions, &c., they
instantly set out again, and again return with cargoes
of Christians and their effects. If it sometimes
happens more particularly in winter, that they have
roamed about for any considerable time without light-
ing on any booty, they retire to some one of these
seven places, viz :—If they had been in the west their

the hold less it should interfere with the " dressing " of the oars. The
weapons were never hung, but securely lashed, and when chasing an
enemy, no movement of any kind was permitted to the crew and
soldiers, save when necessary to the progress and defence of the ship.
These Corsairs, in fact, understood the conditions of a rowing-race to
perfection.

retreats were Tetwān, Al-Araish, or Yusale; those who came from the Spanish coasts went to the island Formentara; and such as had been eastward retired to the island S. Pedro, near Sardinia, the mouths of Bonifacio in Corsica, or the islands Lipari and Strombolo, near Sicily and Calabria; and there, what with the conveniency of those commodious ports and harbours, and the fine springs and fountains of water, with the plenty of wood for fuel they meet with, added to the careless negligence of the Christian galleys, who scarce think it their business to seek for them—they there, very much at their ease, regale themselves, with stretched-out legs, waiting to intercept the paces of Christian ships, which come there and deliver themselves into their clutches." [1]

Father Dan describes their mode of attack as perfectly ferocious. Flying a foreign flag, they lure the unsuspecting victim within striking distance, and then the gunners (generally renegades) ply the shot with unabated rapidity, while the sailors and boatswains chain the slaves that they may not take part in the struggle. The fighting men stand ready, their arms bared, muskets primed, and scimitars flashing, waiting for the order to board. Their war-cry was appalling; and the fury of the onslaught was such as to strike panic into the stoutest heart.

When a prize was taken the booty was divided with scrupulous honesty between the owners and the captors, with a certain proportion (varying from a fifth to an eighth) reserved for the Beylik, or government, who also claimed the hulks. Of the remainder, half

[1] HAEDO, 17.

went to the owners and reïs, the other half to the crew and soldiers. The principal officers took each three shares, the gunners and helmsmen two, and the soldiers and swabbers one; the Christian slaves received from 1½ to three shares apiece. A scrivener saw to the accuracy of the division. If the prize was a very large one, the captors usually towed it into Algiers at once, but small vessels were generally sent home under a lieutenant and a jury-crew of Moors.

There is no mistaking the aspect of a Corsair who has secured a prize : for he fires gun after gun as he draws near the port, utterly regardless of powder. The moment he is in the roads, the *Liman* Reïs, or Port Admiral, goes on board, and takes his report to the Pasha ; then the galleot enters the port, and all the oars are dropped into the water and towed ashore, so that no Christian captives may make off with the ship in the absence of the captain and troops. Ashore all is bustle and delighted confusion ; the dulness of trade, which is the normal condition of Algiers between the arrivals of prizes, is forgotten in the joy of renewed wealth ; the erstwhile shabby now go strutting about, pranked out in gay raiment, the commerce of the bar-rooms is brisk, and every one thinks only of enjoying himself. Algiers is *en fête.*

XVII.

THE TRIUMPH OF SAILS.

17th Century.

AT the beginning of the seventeenth century a notable
change came over the tactics of the Corsairs : they
built fewer galleys, and began to construct square-
sailed ships. In Algiers, Tunis, and Tripoli the
dockyards teemed with workmen busily engaged in
learning the new build ; and the honour, if such it
be, of having taught them rests apparently between
England and Flanders. Simon Danser, the Flemish
rover, taught the Algerines the fashion of "round
ships," in 1606, and an Englishman seems to have
rendered the same kind office to the people of Tunis,
aided by a Greek renegade, Memi Reïs ; where, moreover, another English pirate, "Captain Wer," was
found in congenial company at the Goletta by
Monsieur de Breves, the French ambassador.[1] The
causes of the change were twofold : first, Christian
slaves were not always to be caught, and to hire
rowers for the galleys was a ruinous expense ; and
secondly, the special service for which the smaller
galleots and brigantines were particularly destined,

[1] DAN, Bk. III., ch. iv., p. 273–5, 280.

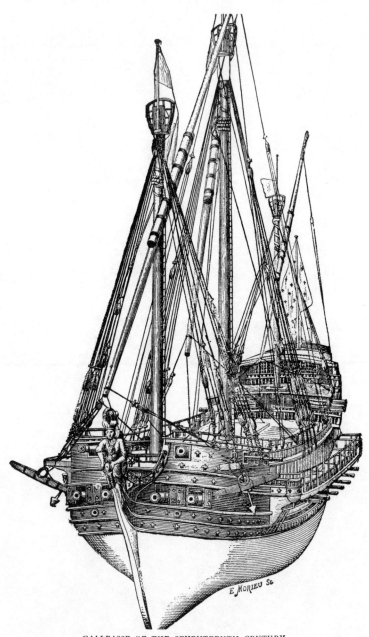

GALLEASSE OF THE SEVENTEENTH CENTURY.

(*Jurien de la Gravière.*)

the descents upon the Spanish coasts was to some
degree obstructed by the final expulsion of the last of
the Moors from Andalusia in 1610.[1] That stroke
deprived the Corsairs of the ready guides and
sympathisers who had so often helped them to
successful raids, and larger vessels and more fighting
men were needed if such descents were to be continued. Moreover, the Barbary rovers were ambitious
to contend with their old enemies for golden treasure
on the Spanish main itself? the science of navigation
was fast developing; and they felt themselves as
equal to venturing upon long cruises as any European
nation. Now a long cruise is impossible in a galley,
where you have some hundreds of rowers to feed, and
where each pound of biscuit adds to the labour of
motion ; but sails have no mouths, and can carry
along a great weight of provisions without getting
tired, like human arms. So sails triumphed over
oars. The day of the galley was practically over,
and the epoch of the ship had dawned. As early as
1616 Sir Francis Cottington reported to the Duke of
Buckingham that the sailing force of Algiers was
exciting general alarm in Spain : " The strength and
boldness of the Barbary pirates is now grown to that
height, both in the ocean and the Mediterranean seas,
as I have never known anything to have wrought a
greater sadness and distraction in this Court than the
daily advice thereof. Their whole fleet consists of
forty sail of tall ships, of between two and four
hundred tons a piece ; their admiral [flagship] of five
hundred. They are divided into two squadrons ; the

---

[1] See the *S'ory of the Moors in Spain*, 279.

on: of eighteen sail remaining before Malaga, in sight
of the city ; the other about the Cape of S. Maria,
which is between Lisbon and Seville.   That squadron
within the straits entered the road of Mostil, a town
by Malaga, where with their ordnance they beat down
part of the castle, and had doubtless taken the town,
bit that from Granada there came soldiers to succour
it ; yet they took there divers ships, and among them
three or four from the west part of England.   Two
big English ships they drove ashore, not past four
leagues from Malaga ; and after they got on shore
also, and burnt them, and to this day they remain
before Malaga, intercepting all ships that pass that way,
and absoluting prohibiting all trade into those parts
of Spain."   The other squadron was doing the same
thing outside the straits, and the Spanish fleet was
both too small in number and too cumbrous in build
to attack them successfully.   Yet " if this year they
safely return to Algiers, especially if they should take
any of the fleet, it is much to be feared that the King
of Spain's forces by sea will not be sufficient to
restrain them hereafter, so much sweetness they find
by making prize of all Christians whatsoever."

This dispatch shows that the Corsairs had speedily
mastered the new manner of navigation, as might
have been expected of a nation of sailors.   They had
long been acquainted with the great galleasse of
Spain and Venice, a sort of compromise between the
rowed galley and the sailing galleon ; for it was too
heavy to depend wholly on its oars (which by way of
distinction were rowed under cover), and its great
lateen sails were generally its motive power.   The

galleys themselves, moreover, had sails, though not
square sails; and the seaman who can sail a ship
on lateen sails soon learns the management of
the square rig. The engravings on pp. 5, 11, 165,
197, and 227 sufficiently show the type of vessel
that now again came into vogue, and which was
known as a galleon, nave, polacca, tartana, bar-
cone, caravel, caramuzel, &c., according to its size
and country. The Turkish caramuzel or tartan,
says Furttenbach, stands high out of the water,
is strong and swift, and mounts eighteen or
twenty guns and as many as sixty well-armed
pirates. It is a dangerous vessel to attack. From
its commanding height its guns can pour down so
furious a fire upon a Christian craft that the only
alternative to surrender is positive extirpation. If
the enemy tries to sneak out of range below the level
of fire, the Turks drop grenades from the upper decks
and set the ship on fire, and even if the Christians
succeeded in boarding, they find themselves in a
trap : for though the ship's waist is indeed cleared of
the enemy, the hurricane decks at poop and prow
command the boarding party, and through loopholes
in the bulwarks—as good a cover as a trench—a
hail of grape pours from the guns, and seizing
their opportunity the Turks rush furiously through
the doors and take their opponents simultaneously
in face and rear; and then comes a busy time for
scimitar and pike. Or, when you are alongside, if
you see the caramuzel's mainsail being furled, and
something moving in the iron cage on the *gabia* or
maintop, know that a petard will soon be dropped in

your midst from the main peak, and probably a heavy stone or bomb from the opposite end of the long lateen yard, where it serves the double purpose of missile and counterpoise. Now is the time to keep your distance, unless you would have a hole in your ship's bottom. The Corsairs, indeed, are very wily

ANCHOR.

in attack and defence, acquainted with many sorts of projectiles,—even submarine torpedoes, which a diver will attach to the enemy's keel,— and they know how to serve their stern chasers with amazing accuracy and rapidity.[1]

With their newly-built galleons, the raids of the Corsairs became more extensive : they were no longer bounded by the Straits of Gibraltar, or a little outside ; they pushed their successes north and south. In 1617 they passed the Straits with eight well-armed vessels and bore down upon Madeira, where they landed eight hundred Turks. The scenes that followed were of the usual character ; the whole island was laid waste, the churches pillaged, the people abused and enslaved. Twelve hundred men, women, and children were brought back to Algiers,

[1] FURTTENBACH, *Architectura Navalis*, 107–110.

with much firing of guns, and other signals of joy, in
which the whole city joined.

In 1627 Murād—a German renegade—took three
Algerine ships as far north as Denmark and Iceland,
whence he carried off four hundred, some say eight
hundred, captives ; and, not to be outdone, his name-
sake Murād Reïs, a Fleming, in 1631, ravaged the
English coasts, and passing over to Ireland, descended
upon Baltimore, sacked the town, and bore away two
hundred and thirty-seven prisoners, men, women, and
children, even from the cradle. " It was a piteous
sight to see them exposed for sale at Algiers," cries
good Father Dan ; "for then they parted the wife
from the husband, and the father from the child ;
then, say I, they sell the husband here, and the wife
there, tearing from her arms the daughter whom she
cannot hope to see ever again." [1] Many bystanders
burst into tears as they saw the grief and despair of
these poor Irish.

As before, but with better confidence, they pursue
their favourite course in the Levant, and cruize across
the Egyptian trade route, where are to be caught
ships laden with the products of Cairo and San'a and
Bombay ; and lay-to at the back of Cyprus to snare
the Syrian and Persian goods that sail from Scan-
derūn ; and so home, with a pleasant raid along the
Italian coasts, touching perhaps at an island or two
to pick up slaves and booty, and thus to the mole of
Algiers and the welcome of their mates ; and this in
spite of all the big ships of Christendom, " *qu'ils ne
cessent de troubler, sans que tant de puissantes galeres*

[1] DAN, *Hist. de Barbarie*, 277.

et tant de bons navires que plusieurs Princes Chrestiens tiennent dans leur havres leur donnent la chasse, si ce ne sont les vaisseaux de Malte ou de Ligorne." [1]   And since 1618, when the Janissaries first elected their own Pasha, and practically ignored the authority of the Porte, the traditional fellowship with France, the Sultan's ally, had fallen through, and French vessels now formed part of the Corsairs' quarry.   Between 1628 and 1634, eighty French ships were captured, worth, according to the reïses' valuation, 4,752,000 livres, together with 1,331 slaves.   The King of France must have regretted even the days when Barbarossa wintered at Toulon, so great was the plague of the sea-rovers and apparently so hopeless the attempt to put them down.

[1] DAN, *l. c.,* 278.

XVIII

17th and 18th Centuries.

WHEN galleys went out of fashion, and "round ships" took their place, it may be supposed that the captivity of Christian slaves diminished. In reality, however, the number of slaves employed on the galleys was small compared with those who worked on shore. If the Spanish historian be correct in his statement that at the close of the sixteenth century the Algerines possessed but thirty-six galleys and galleots, (the brigantines were not rowed by slaves,) with a total of twelve hundred oars, even allowing three men to an oar, which is excessive for some of the Corsairs' light galleots, the number of slaves is but three thousand six hundred. But in 1634 Father Dan found twenty-five thousand Christian slaves in the city of Algiers and roundabout, without counting eight thousand renegades, and so far was the fleet from being diminished (except that there were few galleys) that the priest reckoned no less than seventy sailing cruisers, from large thirty-five and forty-gun ships, to ordinary galleons and polaccas ; and on

August 7th he himself saw twenty-eight of the best
of them sail away in quest of Norman and English
ships, which usually came to Spain at that season to
take in wine, oil, and spices. He adds that Tunis
had then but fourteen polaccas ; Salē thirty very
swift caravels, drawing little water on account of the
harbour bar ; and Tripoli but seven or eight, owing to
the vigilance of the Knights of Malta. Altogether,
the whole Barbary fleet numbered one hundred and
twenty sailing ships, besides about twenty-five
galleys and brigantines.

Father Dan draws a miserable picture of the
captives' life ashore. Nothing of course could equal
the torment of the galley-slaves, but the wretchedness
of the shore-slaves was bad enough. When they were
landed they were driven to the Besistān or slave-
market, where they were put up to auction like the
cattle which were also sold there ; walked up and
down by the auctioneer to show off their paces ; and
beaten if they were lazy or weary or seemed to
" sham." The purchasers were often speculators
who intended to sell again,—" bought for the rise," in
fact ; and " Christians are cheap to day " was a
business quotation, just as though they had been
stocks and shares. The prettiest women were
generally shipped to Constantinople for the Sultan's
choice ; the rest were heavily chained and cast into
vile dungeons in private houses till their work was
allotted them, or into the large prisons or bagnios, of
which there were then six in Algiers, each containing
a number of cells in which fifteen or sixteen slaves
were confined. Every rank and quality of both sexes

TORMENTS OF THE SLAVES.
(*Dan, Hist. de Barbarie,* 1637.)

TORMENTS OF THE SLAVES.
(*Dan, Hist. de Barbarie,* 1637.)

might be seen in these wretched dens, gentle and simple, priest and laic, merchant and artisan, lady and peasant-girl, some hopeful of ransom, others despairing ever to be free again. The old and feeble were set to sell water ; laden with chains, they led a donkey about the streets and doled out water from the skin upon his back ; and an evil day it was when the poor captive did not bring home to his master the stipulated sum. Others took the bread to the bake-house and fetched it back in haste, for the Moors love hot loaves. Some cleaned the house, (since Mohammedans detest dirt,) whitened the walls, washed the clothes, and minded the children ; others took the fruit to market, tended the cattle, or laboured in the fields, sometimes sharing the yoke of the plough with a beast of burden. Worst of all was the sore labour of quarrying stone for building, and carrying it down from the mountains to the shore.

Doubtless Father Dan made the worst of the misery he saw : it was not to the interest of the owners to injure their slaves, who might be ransomed or re-sold, and, at any rate, were more valuable in health than in weakness and disease. The worst part of captivity was not the physical toil and blows, but the mental care, the despair of release, the carking ache of proud hearts set to slave for task-masters. Cruelty there certainly was, as even so staunch an apologist for the Moors as Joseph Morgan admits, but it can hardly have been the rule ; and the report of another French priest who visited Algiers and other parts of Barbary in 1719 does not bear out Dan's statements : nor is there any reason to believe that the captives were worse treated in 1634 than in 1719.[1] The latter report, with some of Morgan's comments, may be summarised thus [2] :—

The slaves at Algiers are not indeed so unhappy as those in the hands of the mountain Moors. The policy of those in power, the interests of individuals, and the more sociable disposition of the townspeople, make their lot in general less rigorous : still they are slaves, hated for their religion, overtaxed with work, and liable to apostasy. They are of two sorts : Beylik or Government slaves, and those belonging to private persons. When a Corsair has taken a prize

[1] If one may draw an analogy from Morocco, the Christian slaves there appear to have been well treated in 1728, certainly better than the renegades. They had a Christian Alcaid, were allowed to keep taverns, and were lodged in a tolerable inn, where the Moslems were not allowed to come near them ; they were nursed when sick by Spanish friars (who paid the Emperor of Morocco for the privilege of curing his slaves) ; and many of them amassed fortunes, and kept servants and mules. At least so says BRAITHWAITE, *Hist. of the Rev. in Morocco*, 343 ff.

[2] This is the standard account of Christian slavery under the Corsairs. It is contained in the anonymous work entitled *Seve al Voyages to Barbary*, &c., [translated and annotated by J. Morgan,] second ed., London, Olive Payne, &c., 1736. It is singular that although Sir R. LAMBERT PLAYFAIR's account of the slaves in his *Scourge of Christendom* (1884) p.9 ff. is practically taken verbatim from this work, there is not a word to show his indebtedness. The name of Joseph Morgan is never mentioned in the *Scourge of Christendom*, though the author was clearly indebted to him for various incidents, and among others for a faultily copied letter (p. 35) from the well-known ambassador Sir Francis Cottington (whom Sir R. L. Playfair calls Cotting*ham*). A good many errors in the *Scourge of Christendom* are due to careless copying of unacknowledged writers : such as calling Joshua Bushett of the Admiralty, " Mr. Secretary Bushell," or Sir John Stuart, " Stewart," or eight bells "eight boats," or Sir Peter Denis, " Sir Denis," or misreckoning the ships of Sir R. Mansell's expedition, or turning San Lucar into " St. Lucas."

and has ascertained, by the application of the bastinado, the rank or occupation and proficiency of the
various captives, he brings them before the governor
to be strictly examined as to their place in the
captured vessel, whether passengers or equipage : if
the former, they are claimed by their consuls, who
attend the examination, and as a rule they are set
free ; but if they served on board the ship for pay
they are enslaved.   Drawn up in a row, one in eight
is chosen by the Dey for his own share, and he
naturally selects the best workmen, and the surgeons
and ship's masters, who are at once sent to the
Government bagnio.   The rest are to be divided
equally between the owners and the equipage, and are
taken to the Besistān and marched up and down by
the *dellāls* or auctioneers, to the time of their merits
and calling, till the highest bid is reached.   This is,
however, a merely formal advance, for the final sale
must take place at the Dey's palace, whither the
captives and their would-be purchasers now resort.
The second auction always realizes a much higher
sum than the first ; but the owners and equipage are
only permitted to share the former price, while, by
a beautifully simple process, the whole difference
between the first and second sales goes absolutely to
the Government.

The Government slaves wear an iron ring on one
ankle, and are locked up at night in the bagnios, while
by day they do all the heavy work of the city, as
cleaning, carrying, and quarrying stone.   Their rations
are three loaves a day.   Some have been seen to toil
in chains.   They have nevertheless their privileges ;

they have no work to do on Fridays, and they are at free liberty to play, work, or steal for themselves every day for about three hours before sunset, and Morgan adds that they do steal with the coolest impunity, and often sell the stolen goods back to the owners, who dare not complain. Sometimes the Dey sends them to sea, when they are allowed to retain part of the spoil ; and others are permitted to keep taverns for renegades and the general riff-raff, both of Turks and Christians, to carouze in. Sometimes they may save enough to re-purchase their freedom, but it often happened that a slave remained a slave by preference, sooner than return to Europe and be beggared, and many of them were certainly better off in slavery at Algiers, where they got a blow for a crime, than in Europe, where their ill-deeds would have brought them to the wheel, or at least the halter.

There were undoubtedly instances, however, of unmitigated barbarity in the treatment of prisoners. For example, the Redemptionists relate the sufferings of four Knights of Malta—three of them French gentlemen, and one from Lucca—who were taken captive at the siege of Oran in 1706, and taken to Algiers. Here they were thrust into the Government prison, along with other prisoners and slaves, to the number of two thousand. Faint with the stench, they were removed to the Kasaba or Castle, where they remained two years. News was then brought that the galleys of Malta had captured the *capitana* or flagship of Algiers, with six hundred and fifty Turks and Moors aboard, besides Christian slaves, to say nothing of killed and wounded : whereupon, furiously incensed, the Dey sent the imprisoned knights to the castle dungeon, and loaded them with chains weighing 120 lbs. ; and there they remained, cramped with the irons, in a putrid cavern swarming with rats and other vermin. They could hear the people passing in the street without, and they clanked their chains if so be they might be heard, but none answered. At last their condition came to the ears of the French consul, who threatened like penalties to Turkish prisoners in Malta unless the knights were removed ; and the Dey, on this, lightened their chains by half, and put them in a better room. There these unhappy gentlemen remained for eight long years more, save only at the great festivals of the Church, when they were set free to join in the religious rites at the French consulate ; and once they formed a strange and sad feature in the wedding festivities of the consul, when they assumed their perukes and court-dresses for the nonce, only to exchange them again for the badge of servitude when the joyful moment of liberty was over. Their treatment grew worse as time wore on ; they were made even to drag trucks of stone these knights of an heroic Order ; and hopeless of obtaining so large a sum as nearly $40,000, which was demanded for their ransom, they managed to file their chains and escape to the shore. But there, to their dismay, the ship they expected was not to be seen, and they took refuge with a *marabut* or saint. Much to his credit, this worthy Moslem used his vast spiritual influence for their protection, and the Dey spared their lives. At last, by the joint efforts of their friends and the

Redemptionists, these poor gentlemen were ransomed and restored to their own country.[1]

Among those who endured captivity in Algiers was one whom genius has placed among the greatest men of all time. In 1575, Cervantes [2] was returning from Naples—after serving for six years in the regiment of Figueroa, and losing the use of his left arm at Lepanto —to revisit his own country; when his ship *El Sol* was attacked by several Corsair galleys commanded by Arnaut Memi; and, after a desperate resistance, in which Cervantes took a prominent part, was forced to strike her colours. Cervantes thus became the captive of a renegade Greek, one Deli Memi, a Corsair reïs, who, finding upon him letters of recommendation from persons of the highest consequence, Don John of Austria among them, concluded that he was a prisoner of rank, for whom a heavy ransom might be asked. Accordingly the future author of *Don Quixote* was loaded with chains and harshly treated, to make him the more anxious to be ransomed. The ransom, however, was slow in coming, and meanwhile the captive made several daring, ingenious, but unsuccessful attempts to escape, with the natural consequences or stricter watch and greater severities. At last, in the second year of his captivity, he was able to let

[1] *Several Voyages*, 58–65.

[2] This brief account of Cervantes' captivity is abridged from my friend Mr. H. E. Watts's admirable *Life*, prefixed to his translation of *Don Quixote*. The main original authority on the matter is Haedo, who writes on the evidence of witnesses who knew Cervantes in Algiers, and who one and all spoke with enthusiasm and love of his courage and patience, his good humour and unselfish devotion (WATTS, i. 76, 96).

his friends know of his condition ; whereupon his father strained every resource to send a sufficient sum to release Miguel, and his brother Rodrigo, who was in the like plight. The brother was set free, but Cervantes himself was considered too valuable for the price.

With the help of his liberated brother he once more concerted a plan of escape. In a cavern six miles from Algiers, where he had a friend, he concealed by degrees forty or fifty fugitives, chiefly Spanish gentlemen, and contrived to supply them with food for six months, without arousing suspicion. It was arranged that a Spanish ship should be sent by his brother to take off the dwellers in the cave, whom Cervantes now joined. The ship arrived ; communications were already opened ; when some fishermen gave the alarm ; the vessel was obliged to put to sea ; and, meanwhile, the treachery of one of the captives had revealed the whole plot to Hasan Pasha, the Viceroy, who immediately sent a party of soldiers to the cavern. Cervantes, with his natural chivalry, at once came to the front and took the whole blame upon himself. Surprised at this magnanimity, the Viceroy — who is described in *Don Quixote* as " the homicide of all human kind " [1]—sent for him, and found him as good as his word. No threats of torture or death could extort from him a syllable which could implicate any one of his fellow-

---

[1] *Don Quixote*, I., chap. xl. (WATTS) : " Every day he hanged a slave ; impaled one ; cut off the ears of another ; and this upon so little animus, or so entirely without cause, that the Turks would own he did it merely for the sake of doing it, and because it was his nature."

captives. His undaunted manner evidently overawed
the Viceroy, for instead of chastizing he purchased
Cervantes from his master for five hundred gold
crowns.

Nothing could deter this valiant spirit from his
designs upon freedom. Attempt after attempt had
failed, and still he tried again. Once he was very
near liberty, when a Dominican monk betrayed
him ; even then he might have escaped, if he would
have consented to desert his companions in the plot :
but he was Cervantes. He was within an ace of
execution, thanks to his own chivalry, and was kept
for five months in the Moor's bagnio, under strict
watch, though without blows—no one ever struck him
during the whole of his captivity, though he often
stood in expectation of impalement or some such
horrible death. At last, in 1580, just as he was being
taken off, laden with chains, to Constantinople,
whither Hasan Pasha had been recalled, Father Juan
Gil effected his ransom for about £100 of English
money of the time, and Miguel de Cervantes, after
five years of captivity, was once more free. As has
been well said, if *Don Quixote* and all else of his had
never been written, " the proofs we have here of his
greatness of soul, constancy, and cheerfulness, under
the severest of trials which a man could endure, would
be sufficient to ensure him lasting fame." [1]

Slavery in private houses, shops, and farms, was
tolerable or intolerable according to the character and
disposition of the master and of the slaves. Some

[1] H. E. WATTS, *Life of Cervantes,* prefixed to his translation of *Don
Quixote,* i. 96.

FATHERS OF THE REDEMPTION.

(Dan, *Hist. de Barbarie*, 1637.)

were treated as members of the family, save in their
liberty, as is the natural inclination of Moslems
towards the slaves of their own religion ; others were
cursed and beaten, justly or unjustly, and lived a
dog's life. Those who were supposed to be able to
pay a good ransom were for a time especially ill-
treated, in the hope of compelling them to send for
their money. Escape was rare : the risk was too
great, and the chances too small.

Thousands of Christian slaves meant tens of thousand of Christian sympathisers, bereaved parents and
sisters, sorrowing children and friends ; and it is easy
to imagine what efforts were made to procure the
release of their unhappy relatives in captivity. At
first it was extremely difficult to open negotiations
with the Corsairs ; but when nation after nation
appointed consuls to watch over their interests at
Algiers and Tunis, there was a recognized medium
of negotiation of which the relations took advantage.
As will presently be seen, the office of consul in those
days carried with it little of the power or dignity that
becomes it now, and the efforts of the consul were
often abortive.

There were others than consuls, however, to help
in the good work. The freeing of captives is a
Christian duty, and at the close of the twelfth century Jean de Matha, impressed with the unhappy fate
of the many Christians who languished in the lands
of the infidels, founded the " Order of the Holy
Trinity and Redemption of Captives." The convent
of S. Mathurin at Paris was immediately bestowed
upon the Order, another was built at Rome on the

Coelian Hill, another called Cerfroy near Meaux, and others in many countries, even as far as the Indies. Pope Innocent the Third warmly supported the pious design, and wrote a Latin letter recommending the Redemptionists to the protection of the Emperor of Morocco : it was addressed, *Illustri Miramomolin, Regi Marochetanorum.* Matha's first voyage (1199) brought back one hundred and eighty-six captives, and in succeeding generations some twenty thousand slaves were rescued by the good fathers, who, clad in their white robes, with the blue and red cross on the breast —three colours symbolical of the Three Persons— fearlessly confronted the Corsairs and bartered for the captives' ransom.

Father Pierre Dan and his colleagues of the Order of the Redemption set out from Marseilles, in 1634, in the suite of Sanson le Page, premier herald of France, and conversant in the Turkish tongue, to arrange for the exchange of captives.[1] Some Turks confined in the galleys at Marseilles were to be re-leased in return for the freeing of the three hundred and forty-two Frenchmen who were in captivity in Algiers. The good father's views upon the origin of the Corsairs were very pronounced. He held that they were descended from Ham, the traitor, and were in-heritors of the curse of the patriarch Noah ; further, that

[1] *Histoire de Barbarie et de ses Corsaires*, par le R. P. Fr. PIERRE DAN, Ministre et Superieur du Convent de la Sainte Trinité et Redemp-tion des Captifs, fondé au Chasteau de Fontaine-bleau, et Bachelier en Theologie, de la Faculté de Paris.

A Paris, chez Pierre Rocolet, Libraire et Imprimeur ord^re du Roy, au Palais, aux Armes du Roy et de la Ville. Avec Privilege de sa Majesté. 1637.

they were the cruellest of all the unnatural monsters that Africa has bred, the most barbarous of mankind, pests of the human race, tyrants over the general liberty, and the wholesale murderers of innocent blood. He did not stop to examine into the condition of the galley-slaves in the ports of his own France, or to inquire whether the word Corsair applied to Moslems alone.

On July 15, 1634, Sanson and the priests arrived at Algiers. A full divan was being held, and the Pasha received them courteously, despite their obstinate refusal to dip the French flag to his crescent. They were forced, in deference to the universal custom at Algiers, to surrender their rudder and oars, not so much to prevent their own unauthorized departure, as to remove the temptation of Christian captives making their escape in the vessel. Orders were given that every respect was to be paid to the envoy's party on pain of decapitation. Rooms were prepared for them in the house of the agent who represented the coral fisheries of the neighbouring Bastion de France ; and here Father Dan made an altar, celebrated Mass, and heard confession of the captives. Two days after their arrival, a new Pasha appeared from Constantinople : he was met by two state-galleys, and saluted by the fifteen hundred guns in the forts and the forty galleys in the harbour. The Aga of the Janissaries, and the Secretary of State, with a large suite of officers, drummers, and fifes, received him on his landing with a deafening noise. The new Pasha, who was robed in white, then mounted a splendid barb, richly caparisoned with precious stones and silk embroidery, and rode to

the palace, whence he sent the French envoy a present
of an ox, six sheep, twenty-four fowls, forty-eight hot
loaves, and six dozen wax candles ; to which the Sieur
le Page responded with gold and silver watches,
scarlet cloth, and rich brocades.

Despite these civilities, the negotiations languished ;
and finally, after three months of fruitless endeavours,
the Mission left " this accursed town " in such haste
that they never even looked to see if the wind would
serve them, and consequently soon found themselves
driven by a Greek Levant, or east wind, to Majorca ;
then across to Bujēya, which was no longer a place of
importance or of piracy, since the Algerines had con-
centrated all their galleys at their chief port ; and
then sighted Bona, which showed traces of the invasion of 1607, when six Florentine galleys, commanded
by French gentlemen, had seized the fort, made mince-
meat of the unfortunate garrison, and carried off
eighteen hundred men, women, and children to Le-
ghorn. At last, with much toil, they reached La Calle,
the port of the Bastion de France, a fine castle built
by the merchants of Marseilles in 1561 for the protection of the valuable coral fisheries, and containing
two handsome courts of solid masonry, and a population of four hundred French people. Sanson
Napolon had been governor here, but he was killed
in an expedition to Tabarka ; Le Page accordingly
appointed a lieutenant, and then the Mission returned
to Marseilles, without results. The fathers, however,
soon afterwards sailed for Tunis, whence they brought
back forty-two French captives, with whom they made
a solemn procession, escorted by all the clergy of

Marseilles, and sang a triumphant *Te Deum*, the captives marching joyfully beside them, each with an illustrative chain over his shoulder.

This is but one example of a long course of determined efforts of the Redemptionists (to say nothing of Franciscans and Dominicans) to rescue their unhappy countrymen. In 1719 Father Comelin and others brought away ninety-eight Frenchmen,[1] and similar expeditions were constantly being made. The zeal of the Order was perhaps narrow: we read that when they offered to pay 3,000 pieces for three French captives, and the Dey voluntarily threw in a fourth without increasing the price, they refused the addition because he was a Lutheran. Nevertheless, they worked much good among the Catholic prisoners, established hospitals and chapels in various parts of the Barbary coast, and many a time suffered the penalty of their courage at the hands of a merciless Dey, who would sometimes put them to a cruel death in order to satisfy his vengeance for some reverse sustained by his troops or ships from the forces of France. Catholic, and especially French, captives at least had cause to be grateful to the Fathers of the Redemption. Those of the Northern nations fared worse: they had no powerful, widespread Church organization to help them, their rulers took little thought of their misery, and their tears and petitions went unregarded for many a long year.

[1] *Several Voyages to Barbary*, second ed., Lond., 1736.

XIX.

THE ABASEMENT OF EUROPE.

16th to 18th Centuries.

IT is not too much to say that the history of the foreign relations of Algiers and Tunis is one long indictment, not of one, but of all the maritime Powers of Europe, on the charge of cowardice and dishonour. There was some excuse for dismay at the powerful armaments and invincible seamanship of Barbarossa or the fateful ferocity of Dragut; but that all the maritime Powers should have cowered and cringed as they did before the miserable braggarts who succeeded the heroic age of Corsairs, and should have suffered their trade to be harassed, their lives menaced, and their honour stained by a series of insolent savages, whose entire fleet and army could not stand for a day before any properly generalled force of a single European Power, seems absolutely incredible, and yet it is literally true.

Policy and pre-occupation had of course much to say to this state of things. Policy induced the French to be the friends of Algiers until Spain lost her menacing supremacy; and even later, Louis XIV. is said to have remarked, "If there were no

Algiers, I would make one." Policy led the Dutch
to ally themselves with the Algerines early in the
seventeenth century, because it suited them to see
the lesser trading States preyed upon. Policy sometimes betrayed England into suffering the indignities
of subsidizing a nest of thieves, that the thieving
might be directed against her enemies. Pre-occupation in other struggles—our own civil war, the Dutch
war, the great Napoleonic war—may explain the
indifference to insult or patience under affront which
had to be displayed during certain periods. But
there were long successions of years when no such
apology can be offered, when no cause whatever can
be assigned for the pusillanimity of the governments
of Europe but sheer cowardice, the definite terror of
a barbarous Power which was still believed to possess
all the boundless resources and all the unquenchable
courage which had marked its early days.

Tunis as much as Algiers was the object of the
servile dread of Europe. The custom of offering
presents, which were really bribes, only died out fifty
years ago, and there are people who can still remember the time when consuls-general were made to
creep into the Bey's presence under a wooden bar.[1]
One day the Bey ordered the French consul to kiss
his hand ; the consul refused, was threatened with
instant death, and—kissed it (1740). When in 1762
an English ambassador came in a King's ship to
announce the accession of George III., the Bey made
the same order, but this time it was compromised by
some of the officers kissing his hand instead of their

[1] BROADLEY, *Tunis*, i. 51.

chief. Austria was forced to sue for a treaty, and had to pay an annual tribute (1784). The Danes sent a fleet to beg leave to hoist their flag over their consulate in Tunis : the Bey asked fifteen thousand sequins for the privilege, and the admiral sailed away in despair. After the Venetians had actually defeated the Tunisians several times in the war of 1784-92, Venice paid the Bey Hamuda forty thousand sequins and splendid presents for the treaty of peace. About the same time Spain spent one hundred thousand piastres for the sake of immunity from piracy ; and in 1799 the United States bought a commercial treaty for fifty thousand dollars down, eight thousand for secret service, twenty-eight cannon, ten thousand balls, and quantities of powder, cordage, and jewels. Holland, Sweden, Denmark, Spain, and the United States were tributaries of the Bey !

Yet we have it on the authority of the Redemptionist Fathers, who were not likely to underestimate their adversaries, that in 1719 the Algerines who, "among all the Barbary maritime Powers are much the strongest," had but twenty-five galleons of eighteen to sixty guns, besides caravels and brigantines ; and it appears they were badly off for timber, especially for masts, and for iron, cordage, pitch, and sails. " It is surprising to see in what good condition they keep their ships, since their country affords not wherewithal to do it. . . . When they can get new timber (brought from Bujēya) sufficient to make a ship's bottom-parts, they finish the remainder with the ruins of prize vessels, which they perfectly well know how to employ to most advantage, and thus find the secret of making very neat new ships and excellent sailers out of old ones."[1] Still twenty-five small frigates were hardly a big enough bugbear to terrify all Europe, let them patch them never so neatly. Nevertheless, in 1712, the Dutch purchased the forbearance of these twenty-five ships by ten twenty-four pounders mounted, twenty-five large masts, five cables, four hundred and fifty barrels of powder, two thousand five hundred great shot, fifty chests of gun barrels, swords, &c., and five thousand dollars. Being thus handsomely armed, the Algerines naturally broke the treaty in three years' time, and the Dutch paid even more for a second truce. So flourished the system of the weak levying blackmail upon the strong.[2]

The period of Europe's abasement began when the Barbary Corsairs were recognized as civilized states to be treated with on equal terms : that is to say, when consuls, ambassadors, and royal letters began to arrive at Tunis or Algiers. This period began soon after Doria's disastrous campaign at Jerba, when the battle of Lepanto had destroyed the prestige of the Ottoman navy, but increased if possible the terror of the ruthless Corsairs. No really serious attempt was made to put down the scourge of the Mediterranean between 1560 and Lord Exmouth's victory in 1816. For nearly all that time the British nation, and most of the other maritime states, were represented at Algiers and Tunis by consular agents. Master John Tipton was the first Englishman to become consul anywhere,

---

[1] *Several Voyages*, 97.   [2] *Ibid.* 104, note.

and he was consul at Algiers, first appointed by the newly-formed Turkey Company about 1580, and in 1585 officially named consul of the British nation by Mr. Harebone, the ambassador of England at the Sublime Porte. The records of the long succession of consuls, and agents, and consuls-general, that followed him are a title-roll of shame. The state of things at almost any point in this span of two hundred and thirty years may be described in few words. A consul striving to propitiate a sullen, ignorant, common soldier, called a Dey ; a Christian king, or government, submitting to every affront put upon his representative, recalling him after mortal insult, and sending a more obsequious substitute with presents and fraternal messages ; and now and then a King's ship, carrying an officer of the King's navy, or an ambassador of the King's Council, irresolutely loitering about the Bay of Algiers trying to mollify a surly despot, or perhaps to experiment in a little meaningless bluster, at which the Dey laughs in his sleeve, or even openly, for he knows he has only to persevere in his demands and every government in Europe will give in. Consuls may pull down their flags and threaten war ; admirals may come and look stern, and even make a show of a broadside or two ; but the Dey's Christian Brother of St. James's or the Tuileries—or their ministers for them—have settled that Algiers cannot be attacked : so loud may he laugh at consul and man-of-war.

To attempt to trace in detail the relations of the Pashas, Deys, and Beys of the three Barbary States, and the Sherifs of Morocco, with the various

European Powers, would be a task at once difficult and wearisome. Those with England will be quite sufficient for the purpose, and here, in regard to Algiers, we have the advantage of following the researches of the Agent and Consul-General there, Sir R. Lambert Playfair, who in his *Scourge of Christendom*,[1] has set forth the principal incidents of British relations with the Dey in great detail, and has authenticated his statements by references to official documents of unimpeachable veracity. The facts which he brings to light in a volume of over three hundred pages can here of course be but slightly touched upon, but the reader may turn to his interesting narrative for such more particular information as space excludes from these pages.

The general results arrived at from a study of Sir Lambert Playfair's researches are painful to English self-respect. It is possible that our consuls were not always wisely chosen, and it was a vital defect in our early consular system that our agents were allowed to trade. Mercantile interests, especially in a Corsair state, are likely to clash with the duties of a consul. Some consuls, moreover, were clearly unfitted for their posts. Of one it is recorded that he drank to excess; another is described as "a litigious limb of the law, who values himself upon having practised his talents in that happy occupation with success, against every man that business or occasion gave him dealings with;" a third is represented as "sitting on his bed, with his sword and a brace of pistols at his side, calling for a clergyman to give him the Sacra-

[1] London : Smith and Elder, 1884.

ments that he may die contented." Still, in the long list of consuls, the majority were honourable, upright men, devoted to their country, and anxious to uphold her interests and rights. How were they rewarded? If their own government resented a single act of the ferocious monster they called the Dey—who was any common Janissary chosen by his comrades [1]—the consul went in fear of his life, nay, sometimes was positively murdered. If he was a strong-minded, courageous man, and refused to stoop to the degradation which was expected of him at the Dey's palace, he could not reckon on support at home ; he might be recalled, or his judgment reversed, or he might even pull down the consular flag only to see it run up again by a more temporising successor, appointed by a government which had already endorsed his own resistance. He might generously become surety for thousands of pounds of ransoms for English captives, and never receive back a penny from home. Whatever happened, the consul was held responsible by the Algerines, and on the arrival of adverse news a threatening crowd would

---

[1] Up to 1618 Algiers was governed by a Pasha directly appointed by the Sultan ; from 1618 the Pasha was chosen by the Janissaries and other militia subject to the veto of the Sultan ; in 1671 the Janissaries first elected a Dey out of their own number, every soldier being eligible, and their Dey soon made the Sultan's Pasha a lay figure ; in 1710 the two offices were united in a Dey chosen by the soldiery. These parvenus were by no means ashamed of their origin or principles. Mohammed Dey (1720), getting into a passion with the French consul, exclaimed with more frankness than courtesy : "My mother sold sheeps' feet, and my father sold neats' tongues, but they would have been ashamed to expose for sale so worthless a tongue as thine." Another time the Dey confessed with dignified *naïveté* to Consul Cole : "The Algerines are a company of rogues—*and I am their Captain !*"

surround his house. Sometimes the consul and every Englishman in Algiers would be seized and thrown into prison, and their effects ransacked, and never a chance of restitution. Many were utterly ruined by the extortions of the Dey and governors. Heavy bribes—called "the customary presents"—had to be distributed on the arrival of each fresh consul; and it is easy to understand that the Dey took care that they did not hold the office too long. The government presents were never rich enough, and the unlucky consul had to make up the deficit out of his own pocket. The Dey would contemptuously hand over a magnificently jewelled watch to his head cook in the presence of the donor; and no consul was received at the Palace until the "customary presents" were received. The presence of a remonstrating admiral in the bay was a new source of danger; for the consul would probably be thrown into prison and his family turned homeless into the streets, while his dragoman received a thousand stripes of the bastinado. When the French shelled Algiers in 1683, the Vicar Apostolic, Jean de Vacher, who was acting as consul, and had worked untiringly among the poor captives for thirty-six years, was, by order of Mezzomorto, with many of his countrymen, blown from the cannon's mouth; [1] and the same thing happened to his successor in 1688, when forty-eight other Frenchmen suffered the same barbarous death. The most humiliating etiquette was observed in the Dey's court: the consul must remove his shoes and sword, and reverently kiss the rascal's hand. The Hon.

[1] *Several Voyages*, 111 ff.

Archibald Campbell Fraser, in 1767, was the first consul who flatly refused to pay this unparalleled act of homage, and he was told, in a few years, that the Dey had no occasion for him, and he might go—as if he were the Dey's servant. "Dear friend of this our kingdom," wrote that potentate to H. M. George III. of England, "I gave him my orders,—and he was insolent!" Mr. Fraser went, but was sent back to be reinstated by a squadron of His Majesty's ships. Admiral Sir Peter Denis sailed into Algiers Bay, and having ascertained that the Dey would not consent to receive Mr. Fraser again, sailed out again. His Majesty's Government expressed themselves as completely satisfied with the admiral's action, and resolved to leave the Dey to his reflections. Finally, in the very next year, King George accepts his friend of Algiers' excuses, and appoints a new consul, specially charged " to conduct himself in a manner agreeable to you." The nation paid a pension of £600 a year to Mr. Fraser as indemnity for its Government's poltroonery.

Every fresh instance of submission naturally swelled the overweening insolence of the Deys. A consul had a Maltese cook: the Dey objected to the Maltese, and took the man by force from the consul's house and sent him away in irons. If the consul objected, he might go too. When Captain Hope, of H.M.S. *Romulus*, arrived at Algiers, he received no salute; the consul was ordered to go aboard, leaving his very linen behind him; and frigate and consul were ordered out of the harbour. Consul Falcon, so late as 1803, was arrested on a trumped-up charge,

and forcibly expelled the city : truly Consul Cart-
wright might describe the consular office of Algiers
as " the next step to the infernal regions." In 1808,
merely because the usual tribute was late, the Danish
consul was seized and heavily ironed, made to sleep
in the common prison, and set to labour with the
slaves. The whole consular body rose as one man
and obtained his release, but his wife died from the
shock. A French consul about the same time died
from similar treatment.

Were all these consuls maltreated for mere obstinacy
about trifles ? The records of piracy will answer that
question. So early as 1582, when England was at
peace with the Porte (and as she continued to be for
220 years), gentlemen of good birth began to find a
voyage in the Mediterranean a perilous adventure.
Two Scottish lairds, the Masters of Morton and Oli-
phant, remained for years prisoners at Algiers. Sir
Thomas Roe, proceeding to his post as ambassador at
Constantinople, said that unless checked the Algerine
pirates will brave even the armies of kings at sea,
and endanger the coasts [which would have been no
new thing], and reported that their last cruise had
brought in forty-nine British vessels, and that there
would soon be one thousand English slaves in Algiers :
the pirates were even boasting that they would go
to England and fetch men out of their beds, as it was
their habit to do in Spain. And indeed it was but a
few years later that they sacked Baltimore in County
Cork, and literally carried out their threat. The
Corsairs' galleons might be sighted at any moment
off Plymouth Hoe or Hartland Point, and the worthy

merchants of Bristol, commercial princes in their way, dared not send their richly laden bottoms to sea for fear of a brush with the enemy.

The Reverend Devereux Spratt was captured off Youghal as he was crossing only from Cork to Bristol, and so distressed was the good man at the miserable condition of many of the slaves at Algiers, that when he was ransomed he yielded to their entreaties and stayed a year or two longer to comfort them with his holy offices.[1] It was ministrations such as his that were most needed by the captives : of bodily ill-treatment they had little to complain, but alienation from their country, the loss of home and friends, the terrible fate too often of wife and children —these were the instruments of despair and disbelief in God's providence, and for such as were thus tormented the clergyman was a minister of consolation. In the sad circle of the captives marriages and baptisms nevertheless took place, and some are recorded in the parish register of Castmell, Lancashire, as having been performed in " Argeir " by Mr. Spratt.

Matters went from bad to worse. Four hundred British ships were taken in three or four years before 1622. Petitions went up to the Houses of Parliament from the ruined merchants of the great ports of England. Imploring letters came in from poor Consul Frizell, who continued to plead for succour for twenty years, and then disappeared, ruined and unaided. Touching petitions reached England from the poor captives themselves,—English seamen and captains,

[1] See his descendant Adm. SPRATT's *Travels and Researches in Crete*, i. 384-7.

or plain merchants bringing home their wealth, now suddenly arrested and stripped of all they possessed : piteous letters from out the very bagnios themselves, full of tears and entreaties for help.   In the fourth decade of the seventeenth century there were three thousand husbands and fathers and brothers in Algerine prisons, and it was no wonder that the wives and daughters thronged the approaches to the House of Commons and besieged the members with their prayers and sobs.

Every now and then a paltry sum was doled out by Government for the ransom of slaves, whose capture was due to official supineness ; and we find the House of Lords subscribing nearly £3,000 for the same object.   In the first quarter of the seventeenth century 240 British slaves were redeemed for £1,200 ; and the Algerines, who looked upon the whole matter in a businesslike spirit, not only were willing to give every facility for their purchase, but even sent a special envoy to the Court of St. James's to forward the negotiations.   Towards the middle of the century a good many more were rescued by Edmond Casson as agent for the Government. Alice Hayes of Edinburgh was ransomed for 1,100 double pesetas (two francs each), Sarah Ripley of London for 800, a Dundee woman for only 200, others for as much as 1,390 ; while men generally fetched about 500.[1]   Sometimes, but very rarely, the captives made their own escape. The story is told by Purchas[2] of four English youths who were left on board a prize, the *Jacob* of Bristol, to help a dozen Turkish captors to navigate her, and

---

[1] PLAYFAIR, 64 ff.   [2] *Voyages*, ii. 887.

who threw the captain overboard, killed three more, drove the rest under hatches, and sold them for a round sum in the harbour of San Lucar by Cadiz. Even more exciting were the adventures of William Okeley, who in 1639 was taken on board the *Mary* bound for the West Indies, when but six days from the Isle of Wight. His master, a Moor, gave him partial liberty, and allowed him to keep a wineshop, in consideration of a monthly payment of two dollars ; and in the cellar of his shop the slave secretly constructed a light canoe of canvas, while the staves of empty winepipes furnished the oars. These he and his comrades smuggled down to the beach, and five of them embarked in the crazy craft, which bore them safely to Majorca. The hardest part was the farewell to two more who were to have accompanied them, but were found to overweight the little boat.

Several other narratives of successful escapes may be read in the volume of voyages published by the Redemptionist Fathers, and translated by Joseph Morgan. One at least is worth quoting :

"A good number, of different nations, but mostly Majorcans, conspired to get away by night with a row-boat [*i.e.*, brigantine] ready for the cruise : they were in all about seventy. Having appointed a place of rendezvous, at dead of night they got down through a sewer into the port : but the dogs, which are there very numerous, ran barking at them ; some they killed with clubs and stones. At this noise, those who were on guard, as well ashore as in the ships, bawled out with all their might, ' Christians ! Christians ! ' They then assembled and ran towards the noise. And forty of the slaves having entered the *fregata*, or row-boat, and being stronger than those who guarded her, they threw them all into the sea ; and it being their business to hasten out of the port, embarrassed with cables of the many ships which then quite filled it, and as they were desirous of taking the shortest cut, they took the resolution of leaping all into the water, hoisting up the boat on their shoulders, and wading with it till clear of all those cables. Spite of the efforts to prevent their design, they made out to sea, and soon reached Majorca. On hearing this the Dey cried out, ' I believe these dogs of Christians will come one day or other and take us out of our houses ! ' " [1]

Ransoms and escapes were more than made up by fresh captures. In 1655, indeed, Admiral Blake, after trying to bring the Tunisians to terms, ran into the harbour of Porto Farina on the 3rd of April, where the fleet of the Bey, consisting of nine vessels, was anchored close in under the guns of the forts and earthworks, and under a heavy fire he burnt every one of them : then proceeding to Algiers, found the city in such consternation that he liberated the whole body of British slaves (English, Scots, Irish, and Channel Islanders) for a trifling sum. Nevertheless, four years later, the Earl of Inchiquin, notorious as " Morough of the Burnings," from his manner of making war, and his son, Lord O'Brien, were caught off the Tagus while engaged in one of those foreign services in which royalists were apt to enlist during the troubles at home, and it took the Earl seven or eight months'

[1] *Several Voyages*, 57-8.

captivity and 7,500 crowns to obtain his release. In the following century the remnant of the brave Hibernian Regiment, on its way from Italy, was surrounded and overcome, to the number of about eighty, and was treated with peculiar barbarity. It was no rare thing to see British ships—once even a sloop of war—brought captive into Algiers harbour, on some pretext of their papers being out of form ; and the number of slaves continued to increase, in spite of the philanthropic efforts of some of the wealthy merchants, like William Bowtell, who devoted themselves to the humane attempt.

Very often it was the captive's own fault that he was taken. Frequently he was serving on a vessel of a power then at war with Algiers. The system of passes for the Mediterranean opened the way to a good deal of knavery ; ships sailed under false colours, or, being themselves at war with Algiers, carried passes purchased from her allies. The Algerines were shy of contracting too many alliances, lest there should be no nation to prey upon, and we read of a solemn debate in the Divan to decide which nation should be broken with, inasmuch as the slave masters were becoming bankrupt from the pacific relations of the State. This was when the cupidity of the Dey had led him to accept a heavy bribe from Sweden in return for his protection, and the Corsairs rushed excitedly to the palace declaring that they had already too many allies : " Neither in the ocean nor narrow sea can we find scarce any who are not French, English, or Dutch ; nothing remains for us to do, but either to sell our ships for fuel, and return to our primitive camel-driving, or to break with one of these nations." [1] Thus there was generally one favoured nation—or perhaps two—to whom the Algerines accorded the special favour of safe-conducts over the Mediterranean, and it was the object of all other traders to borrow or buy these free passes from their happy possessors. The Algerines were not unnaturally incensed at finding themselves cheated by means of their own passes. "As for the Flemings," complained the Corsairs, " they are a good people enough, never deny us anything, nor are they worse than their word, like the French; but they certainly play foul tricks upon us, in selling their passes to other infidels : For ever since we made peace with them, we rarely light on either Swede, Dane, Hamburgher, &c. All have Dutch complexions; all Dutch passes ; all call each other *Hans, Hans,* and all say *Yaw, Yaw !* "

Many of these counterfeit allies carried English seamen, and such, not being under their own colours, were liable to be detained in slavery. So numerous was this class of captives that, although in 1694 it was reported that no Englishmen captured under the British flag remained in slavery in Algiers, there was ample application soon afterwards for Betton's beneficial bequest of over £21,000 for the purpose of ransoming British captives.

Expedition after expedition was sent to argue, to remonstrate, to threaten, with literally no result. Ambassador after ambassador came and went, and made useless treaties, and still the Algerines main-

[1] MORGAN, Pref. v, vi.

tained the preposterous *right to search British vessels*
at sea, and take from them foreigners and goods.
Sir Robert Mansell first arrived in 1620 with eighteen
ships and five hundred guns, manned by 2,600
men ; and accomplished nothing.   As soon as they
turned their backs the pirates took forty British
ships.   Sir Thomas Roe made a treaty, which turned
out to be waste paper.   Blake frightened the Corsairs
for the moment.   The Earl of Winchelsea, in 1660,
admitted the right of search.   Lord Sandwich in the
following year cannonaded Algiers without result
from a safe distance.   Four times Sir Thomas Allen
brought his squadron into the bay, and four times
sailed he out, having gained half his purpose, and
twice his desert of insult: " These men," cried 'Ali
Aga, "talk as if they were drunk, and would force
us to restore their subjects whether they will or no !
Bid them begone." [1]   The only satisfactory event to
be reported after fifty years of fruitless expeditions is
Sir E. Spragg's attack on the Algerine fleet, beached
under the guns of Bujēya : like Blake, he sent in a
fireship and burnt the whole squadron.   Whereupon
the Janissaries rose in consternation, murdered their
Aga, and, carrying his head to the Palace, insisted
on peace with England.

It was a very temporary display of force.   Five
years later Sir John Narborough, instead of bom-
barding, was meekly paying sixty thousand " pieces
of eight" to the Algerines for slaves and presents.
In 1681 Admiral Herbert, afterwards Lord Torring-
ton, executed various amicable cruises against the

[1] PLAYFAIR, 94.

Algerines. In 1684 Sir W. Soame with difficulty extorted a salute of twenty-one guns to His Britannic Majesty's flag. And so the weary tale of irresolution and weakness went on. Admiral Keppel's expedition in 1749 is chiefly memorable for the presence of Sir Joshua Reynolds as a guest on board the flagship ; and it is possible that two sketches reproduced by Sir Lambert Playfair are from his pencil : the drawings were the only fruit of the cruise. James Bruce, the African traveller, as agent or consul-general in 1763, put a little backbone into the communications, but he soon went on his travels, and then the old fruitless course of humble remonstrances and idle demonstrations went on again. Whenever more serious attempts were made, the preparations were totally inadequate. Spain, Portugal, Naples, and Malta sent a combined fleet in 1784 to punish the Algerines, but the vessels were all small and such as the Corsairs could tackle, and so feeble and desultory was the attack that, after a fortnight's fooling, the whole fleet sailed away.

XX.

THE UNITED STATES AND TRIPOLI.

1803-5.

THESE dark days of abasement were pierced by
one ray of sunlight; the United States refused the
tribute demanded by the Barbary Rovers. From its
very birth the new nation had, in common with all
other maritime countries, accepted as a necessary evil
a practice it was now full time to abolish. As early
as 1785 the Dey of Algiers found in American
commerce a fresh field for his ploughing; and of all
traders, none proved so welcome as that which boasted
of its shipping, yet carried not an ounce of shot to
defend it. Hesitating protests and negotiations were
essayed in vain; until at last public opinion was so
aroused by the sufferings of the captives as to demand
of Congress the immediate construction of a fleet.
Ill news travels apace, and the rumours of these preparations echoed so promptly among the white walls
of Algiers, that the Dey hastened to conclude a
treaty; and so, long before the frigates were launched,

immunity was purchased by the payment of a heavy tribute. Like all cowardly compromises, this one shaped itself into a two-edged sword ; and soon every rover from Mogador to the Gates of the Bosphorus was clamouring for *backsheesh*. In 1800, Yūsuf, the Pasha of Tripoli, threatened to slip his falcons upon the western quarry, unless presents, similar to those given by England, France, and Spain, were immediately sent him. He complained that the American Government had bribed his neighbours, the cut-throats of Tunis, at a higher price, and he saw no reason why, like his cousin of Algiers, he should not receive a frigate as hush-money. His answer to a letter of the President, containing honeyed professions of friendship, was amusing. "We would ask," he said, "that these your expressions be followed by deeds, and not by empty words. You will, therefore, endeavour to satisfy us by a good manner of proceeding. . . . But if only flattering words are meant without performance, every one will act as he finds convenient. We beg a speedy answer without neglect of time, as a delay upon your part cannot but be prejudicial to your interests."

The Bey of Tunis made demands no less arrogant. He declared that Denmark, Spain, Sicily, and Sweden had made concessions to him, and then he announced: " It would be impossible to keep peace longer, unless the President sent him without delay ten thousand stand of arms and forty cannons of *different calibre*. And all these last " (he added, with a fine Hibernicism) "must be 24-pounders." Algiers hinted that her money was in arrears, and Morocco intimated that her delay in arranging terms was due simply to the full consideration which she was giving to a matter so important.

Whatever other faults Yūsuf of Tripoli may have had, he was in this matter as good as his word, and the six months' notice having been fruitless, he proclaimed war on May 14, 1801, by chopping down the flagstaff of the American Consulate. But the government of the United States was weary of the old traditions followed by Christendom in its dealings with these swashbucklers. They had by this time afloat a small but effective squadron, and were very proud of the successes it had gained in the *quasi*-war with France just ended. They were tired also of a policy which was utterly at odds with their boast that all men were born free and equal, and the nation was roused with the shibboleth that there were " millions for defence, but not one cent for tribute."

When the excitement had cooled, however, it seemed as if there was as usual to be more in the promise than in the performance, for, though a force existed sufficient for vigorous and decisive action, nothing was accomplished during two years and more. Of the three squadrons sent out, the first, under Dale, was hampered by the narrow restrictions of the President's orders, due to constitutional scruples as to the propriety of taking hostile measures before Congress had declared war ; and the second was unfortunate in its commander, though individual deeds reflected the greatest credit upon many of the subordinate officers. In 1803 the third squadron assembled

at Gibraltar under the broad pennant of Commodore
Edward Preble, and then at last came the time for
vigorous measures.

The flag-officer's objective point was Tripoli, but
hardly were his ships gathered for concerted action,
when the *Philadelphia*, thirty-six guns, captured off
the coast of Spain the *Meshboa*, an armed cruiser
which belonged to Morocco, and had in company as
prize the Boston brig *Celia.* Of course it was of the
highest importance to discover upon what authority
the capture had been made ; but the Moorish commander lied loyally, and swore that he had taken the
Celia in anticipation of a war which he was sure had
been declared, because of the serious misunderstand-
ing existing when he was last in port between his
Emperor and the American consul. This story was
too improbable to be believed, and Captain Bainbridge of the *Philadelphia* threatened to hang as a
common pirate the mendacious Reïs Ibrahīm Lubarez
unless he showed his commission. When the rover
saw this menace did not issue in idleness, he confessed
he had been mistaken, and that he had been ordered by
the Governor of Tangiers to capture American vessels.
This made the matter one which required decisive
action, and so the prize was towed to Gibraltar,
and Preble sailed for Tangiers to demand satisfaction.
There was the usual interchange of paper bullets
and of salutes ; but, in the end, the aggressive Commodore prevailed. The Emperor expressed his regret
for the hostile acts, and disowned them ; he punished
the marauders, released all vessels previously captured,
agreed to ratify the treaty made by his father in 1786,

and added that "his friendship for America should last for ever."

This affair being settled, Preble detailed the *Philadelphia* and *Vixen* for the blockade of Tripoli, and then, as the season was too advanced for further operations, began preparations for the repairs and equipment needed for the next season.

The work assigned to the *Philadelphia* and *Vixen* was rigorous, for the coast—fretted with shoals, reefs, and unknown currents, and harassed by sudden squalls, strong gales, and bad holding grounds— demanded unceasing watchfulness, and rendered very difficult the securing of proper food and ship's stores from the distance of the supplying base. Bad as this was in the beginning, it became worse when in October the *Vixen* sailed eastward in search of a Tripolitan cruiser which was said to have slipped past the line at night, for then the whole duty, mainly in-shore chasing, fell to the deep-draught frigate. It was while thus employed that she came to misfortune, as Cooper writes, in his History of the United States Navy : "Towards the last of October the wind, which had been strong from the westward for some time previously, drove the *Philadelphia* a considerable distance to the eastward of the town, and on Monday, October the 31st, as she was running down to her station again with a fair breeze, about nine in the morning a vessel was seen inshore and to windward, standing for Tripoli. Sail was made to cut her off. Believing himself to be within long gun-shot a little before eleven, and seeing no other chance of over-taking the stranger in the short distance that remained,

Captain Bainbridge opened fire in the hope of cutting something away. For near an hour longer the chase and the fire were continued ; the lead, which was kept constantly going, giving from seven to ten fathoms, and the ship hauling up and keeping away as the water shoaled or deepened. At half-past eleven, Tripoli then being in plain sight, distant a little more than a league, (satisfied that he could neither overtake the chase nor force her ashore,) Captain Bainbridge ordered the helm a-port to haul directly off the land into deep water. The next cast of the lead, when this order was executed, gave but eight fathoms, and this was immediately followed by casts that gave seven and six and a half. At this moment the wind was nearly abeam, and the ship had eight knots way upon her. When the cry of 'half-six' was heard, the helm was put hard down and the yards were ordered to be braced sharp up. While the ship was coming up fast to the wind, and before she had lost her way, she struck a reef forwards, and shot on it until she lifted between five and six feet."

Every effort was made to get her off, but in vain. The noise of the cannonading brought out nine gun-boats ; and then, as if by magic, swarms of wreckers slipped by the inner edge of the shore, stole from some rocky inlet, or rushed from mole and galley, and keeping beyond range, like vultures near a battle-field, awaited the surrender of the ship. A gallant fight was made with the few guns left mounted, but at last the enemy took up a position on the ship's weather quarter, where her strong heel to port forbade the bearing of a single piece. "The gun-boats," continues the his-

torian, " were growing bolder every minute, and night
was at hand. Captain Bainbridge, after consulting
again with his officers, felt it to be an imperious duty
to haul down his flag, to save the lives of his people.
Before this was done the magazines were drowned,
holes were bored in the ship's bottom, the pumps
were choked, and everything was performed that it
was thought would make sure the final loss of the
vessel. About five o'clock the colours were lowered."
The ship was looted, the officers and men were robbed,
half stripped in some cases, and that night the crew
was imprisoned in a foul Tripolitan den. Within a
week the rovers, aided by favourable winds and unusual tides, not only got the *Philadelphia* afloat, but,
as the scuttling had been hastily done, towed her
into port, and weighed all the guns and anchors that
lay in shallow water on the reef. The ship was
immediately repaired, the guns were re-mounted, and
the gallant but unfortunate Bainbridge had the final
misery of seeing his old command safely moored off
the town, and about a quarter of a mile from the
Pasha's castle.

Preble heard of this catastrophe from an English
frigate which he spoke off Sardinia on his way to
Tripoli. The blow was a severe one, for the ship
represented over one-third of his fighting force, and
the great number of captives gave the enemy a
material and sentimental strength which he would be
sure to use pitilessly in all future negotiations. But
the energetic sailor was only stimulated by the
disaster to greater exertions, and plans were immediately made for the destruction of the captured ship.

TRIPOLI.

(*Ogilby's Africa*, 1670.)

Fortunately there was no lack of material, and, in selecting the leaders, it became an embarrassment to decide between the claims of the volunteers. Finally the choice fell upon Lieutenant Stephen Decatur. He was at this time twenty-four years of age, and had by his marked qualities so distinguished himself as to have been appointed to the command of the *Enterprise*. To great prudence, self-control, and judgment, he united the dash, daring, and readiness of resources which have always characterized the famous sailors of the world ; and in the victory which made his name renowned in naval annals, he displayed these qualities in such a high degree as to deserve the greatest credit for what he achieved as well as for what, under great temptation, he declined to do.

After taking on board a load of combustibles, the *Intrepid* sailed from Syracuse for Tripoli upon the 3rd of February, 1804. The ketch itself had a varied history, for she was originally a French gun vessel, which had been captured by the English in Egypt and presented to Tripoli, and which finally was seized by Decatur while running for Constantinople with a present of female slaves for the Grand Vizir. The brig *Siren*, Lieutenant Charles Stewart, commanding, convoyed the expedition, and had orders to cover the retreat, and if feasible to assist the attack with its boats. In affairs of this kind personal comfort is always the least consideration, but had not the weather been pleasant, the hardships endured might seriously have affected the success of the enterprise. The five commissioned officers were crowded in the small cabin ; the midshipmen and pilot on one side, and the seamen upon the other, were stowed like herrings upon " a platform laid across water-casks, whose surface they completely covered when they slept, and at so small a distance below the spar deck that their heads would reach it when seated." To these inconveniences were added the want of any room for exercise on deck, the attacks of innumerable vermin which their prede-cessors, the slaves, had left behind them, and (as the salted meat put on board had spoiled) the lack of anything but biscuits to eat and water to drink.

After a voyage of six days the town was sighted, but strong winds had rendered the entrances dangerous, and the heavy gale which came with night drove the Americans so far to the eastward before it abated that they found themselves fairly embayed in the Gulf of Sidra. On the afternoon of the 16th Tripoli was once more made out; and as the wind was light, the weather pleasant, and the sea smooth, Decatur determined to attack that night. By arrangement the *Siren* kept almost out of sight during the day, and her appearance was so changed as to lull all suspicion of her true character. The lightness of the wind allowed the ketch to maintain the appearance of an anxious desire to reach the harbour before night, without bringing her too near to require any other change than the use of drags (in this case buckets towed astern) which could not be seen from the city. The crew was kept below, excepting six or eight persons at a time, so that inquiry might not be awakened by unusual numbers; and such men remained on deck as were dressed like Maltese. When the *Philadelphia* was sighted, no doubt was left of the hazardous nature of the attack, for she lay a mile within the entrance, riding to the wind and abreast of the town. Her foremast, which was cut away while on the reef, had not yet been replaced, her main and mizzen masts were housed, and her lower yards were on the gunwales. The lower standing rigging, however, was set up, and her battery was loaded and shotted. She lay within short range of the guns on the castle, on the mole-head, and in the New Fort; and close aboard rode three Tripolitan cruisers and twenty gun-boats and galleys. To meet and overcome this force Decatur had a few small guns and seventy men, but these were hearts of oak, tried in many a desperate undertaking, and burning now to redeem their country's honour.

As the *Intrepid* drew in with the land, they saw that the boiling surf of the western passage would force them to select the northern entrance, which twisted and turned between the rocks and the shoals. It was now nearly ten o'clock, and as the ketch drifted in before the light easterly breeze she seemed a modest trader bent upon barter, and laden with anything but the hopes of a nation.

The night was beautiful; a young moon sailed in the sky; the lights from wall and tower and town, and from the ships lazily rocking at the anchorages, filled the water with a thousand points of fire. The gentle breeze wafted the little craft past reefs and rocks into the harbour noiselessly, save for the creaking of the yards, the complainings of the block, the

wimple of wavelets at the bow, and the gurgle of
eddies at the pintles and under the plashing counter.
On deck forward only a few figures were silhouetted
against the background of white wall and grayish
sky ; and aft Decatur and the pilot stood conning
the ship as it stole slowly for the frigate's bow.

Owing to the ketch's native rig, and to the glib
Tripolitanese of the Sicilian pilot, no suspicion was
excited in the *Philadelphia's* watch by the answer to
their hail that she had lost her anchors in a gale and
would like to run a line to the war-ship and to ride
by it through the night. So completely were the
Tripolitans deceived that they lowered a boat and
sent it with a hawser, while at the same time some
of the *Intrepid's* crew leisurely ran a fast to the
frigate's fore-chains. As these returned they met the
enemy's boat, took its rope, and passed it into their
own vessel. Slowly, but firmly, it was hauled upon
by the men on board, lying on their backs, and
slowly and surely the *Intrepid* was warped alongside.
But at the critical moment the ruse was discovered,
and up from the enemies' decks went the wolf-like
howl of " Americanos ! Americanos ! "

The cry roused the soldiers in the forts and batteries, and the chorus these awakened startled the
Pasha from his sleep, and thrilled with joy the
captive Americans behind their prison walls.

In another moment the *Intrepid* had swung broadside on, and quickly-passed lashings held the two
ships locked in a deadly embrace. Then Decatur's
cry of " board " rang out, and with a quick rush, and the
discharge of only a single gun, the decks were gained.

The surprise was as perfect as the assault was rapid, and the Tripolitan crew, panic stricken, huddled like rats at bay awaiting the final dash. Decatur had early gathered his men aft, stood a moment for them to gain a sight of the enemy, and then, with the watchword "*Philadelphia,*" rushed upon the rovers. No defence was made, for, swarming to leeward, they tumbled, in mad affright, overboard; over the bows, through gun-ports, by aid of trailing halliards and stranded rigging, out of the channels, pell-mell by every loop-hole they went—and then, such as could, swam like water-rats for the friendly shelter of the neighbouring war-galleys.

One by one the decks and holds were cleared, and in ten minutes Decatur had possession of the ship, without a man killed, and only one slightly wounded. In the positions selected so carefully beforehand, the appointed divisions assembled and piled up and fired the combustibles. Each party acted by itself, and as it was ready; and so rapid were all in their movements, that those assigned to the after-holds had scarcely reached the cockpit and stern store-rooms before the fires were lighted over their heads. Indeed, when the officer entrusted with this duty had completed his task, he found the after-hatches so filled with smoke from the fire in the ward-room and steerage, that he was obliged to escape to the deck by the forward ladders.

Satisfied that the work was thoroughly done, the Americans leaped upon the *Intrepid's* deck, cut with swords and axes the hawsers lashing them to the *Philadelphia*, manned the sweeps, and, just as the flames were scorching their own yards and bulwarks, swung clear.   Then came the struggle for escape, and this last scene can best be told, perhaps, in the words of one of the participants, Commodore Charles Morriss, who gave on that night, when he was the first to board the *Philadelphia*, the earliest proof of the great qualities which afterwards made him one of the first sailors of his time.   "Up to this time," he wrote, "the ships and batteries of the enemy had remained silent, but they were now prepared to act ; and when the crew of the ketch gave three cheers in exultation of their success, they received the return of a general discharge from the enemy.   The confusion of the moment probably prevented much care in their direction, and though under the fire of nearly a hundred pieces for half an hour, the only shot which struck the ketch was one through the topgallant sail. We were in greater danger from the *Philadelphia*, whose broadsides commanded the passage by which we were retreating, and whose guns were loaded, and discharged as they became heated.   We escaped these also, and while urging the ketch onwards with sweeps, the crew were commenting upon the beauty of the spray thrown up by the shot between us and the brilliant light of the ship, rather than calculating any danger that might be apprehended from the contact. The appearance of the ship was, indeed, magnificent. The flames in the interior illuminated her ports, and, ascending her rigging and masts, formed columns of fire, which, meeting the tops, were reflected into beautiful capitals ; whilst the occasional discharge of her guns gave an idea of some directing spirit within her.

The walls of the city and its batteries, and the masts and rigging of cruisers at anchor, brilliantly illuminated and animated by the discharge of artillery, formed worthy adjuncts and an appropriate background to the picture. Fanned by a light breeze our exertions soon carried us beyond the range of their shot, and at the entrance of the harbour we met the boats of the *Siren*, which had been intended to cooperate with us, and whose crew rejoiced at our success, whilst they grieved at not having been able to partake in it. . . . The success of this enterprise added much to the reputation of the navy, both at home and abroad. Great credit was given, and was justly due to Commodore Preble, who directed and first designed it, and to Lieutenant Decatur, who volunteered to execute it, and to whose coolness, self-possession, resources, and intrepidity its success was, in an eminent degree, due."

Commodore Preble, in the meantime, hurried his preparations for more serious work, and on July 25th arrived off Tripoli with a squadron, consisting of the frigate *Constitution*, three brigs, three schooners, six gunboats, and two bomb vessels. Opposed to him were arrayed over a hundred guns mounted on shore batteries, nineteen gunboats, one ten-gun brig, two schooners mounting eight guns each, and twelve galleys. Between August 3rd and September 3rd five attacks were made, and though the town was never reduced, substantial damage was inflicted, and the subsequent satisfactory peace rendered possible. Preble was relieved by Barron in September, not because of any loss of confidence in his ability, but from exigencies of the service, which forbade the Government sending out an officer junior to him in the relief squadron which reinforced his own. Upon his return to the United States he was presented with a gold medal, and the thanks of Congress were tendered him, his officers, and men, for gallant and faithful services.

The blockade was maintained vigorously, and in 1805 an attack was made upon the Tripolitan town of Derna, by a combined land and naval force; the former being under command of Consul-General Eaton, who had been a captain in the American army, and of Lieutenant O'Bannon of the Marines. The enemy made a spirited though disorganized defence, but the shells of the war-ships drove them from point to point, and finally their principal work was carried by the force under O'Bannon and Midshipman Mann. Eaton was eager to press forward, but he was denied reinforcements and military stores, and much of his advantage was lost. All further operations were, however, discontinued in June, 1805, when, after the usual intrigues, delays, and prevarications, a treaty was signed by the Pasha, which provided that no further tribute should be exacted, and that American vessels should be for ever free of his rovers. Satisfactory as was this conclusion, the uncomfortable fact remains that tribute entered into the settlement. After all the prisoners had been exchanged man for man, the Tripolitan Government demanded, and the United States paid, the handsome sum of sixty thousand dollars to close the contract.

This treaty, however, awakened the conscience of Europe, and from the day it was signed the power of the Barbary Corsairs began to wane. The older countries saw their duty more clearly, and ceased to legalize robbery on the high seas. To America the success gave an immediate position which could not easily have been gained in any other way, and, apart from its moral results, the contest with Tripoli was the most potent factor in consolidating the navy of the United States.

XXI.

THE BATTLE OF ALGIERS

1816.

NELSON was in the Mediterranean at the beginning of the nineteenth century, as every one knows, but the suppression of the Barbary Corsairs formed no part of his instructions. Twice, indeed, he sent a ship of war to inquire into the complaints of the consuls, but without effect; and then on the glorious Twenty-First of October, 1805, the great admiral fell in the supreme hour of victory. Collingwood made no attempt to deal with the Algerine difficulty, beyond sending a civilian agent and a present of a watch, which the Dey consigned to his cook. The British victories appear to have impressed the pirates' mind but slightly; and in 1812 we find Mr. A'Court (Lord Heytesbury) condescending to negotiate terms between the Corsairs and our allies the Portuguese, by which the latter obtained immunity from molestation and the release of their countrymen by the payment altogether of over a million of dollars, and an annual tribute of $24,000.

To the United States of America belongs the

honour of having first set an example of spirited
resistance to the pretensions of the Corsairs. So
long as they had been at war with Great Britain, the
States were unable to protect their commerce in the
Mediterranean ; and they were forced to fall in with
the prevailing custom and make peace with the robbers on the basis of a bribe over a million of Spanish
dollars, and a large annual tribute in money and
naval stores. But as soon as the Treaty of Ghent
set them free in 1815 they sent a squadron to Algiers,
bearing Mr. William Shaler as American consul, and
Captains Bainbridge and Stephen Decatur as his
assessors in the impending negotiations. The result
was that after only two days a Treaty was concluded
on June 30, 1815, by which all money payment was
abolished, all captives and property were restored, and
the United States were placed on the footing of the
most favoured nation. The arguments of the Americans appear to have been more eloquent than British
broadsides.

Shamed by this unexpected success, the English
Government at length sent Lord Exmouth (formerly
Sir Edward Pellew) to obtain favourable terms for
some of the minor Mediterranean Powers, and to
place the Ionian Islands, as British dependencies, on
the same footing as England. Yet he was evidently
not authorized to proceed to extreme measures or
demand unconditional surrender of existing pretensions. He arranged terms for Naples, which still
included tribute and presents. Sardinia escaped for
a sum down. The Ionians were admitted on the
English footing. Then Lord Exmouth went on to

Tunis and Tripoli, and obtained from the two Beys
the promise of the total abolition of Christian slavery.

His proceedings at Tunis were marked by much
firmness, and rewarded with commensurate success.
He arrived on the 12th of April, 1816, shortly after a
Tunisian Corsair, in devastating one of the Sardinian
islands, had roused the indignation of Europe. Lord
Exmouth demanded nothing less than the total
abolition of Christian slavery. " It happened that at
this very time Caroline, Princess of Wales, was
enjoying the splendid hospitality of Mahmūd Bey in
his city palace. Neither party seemed inclined to
yield, and matters assumed a very threatening aspect.
The mediation of the royal guest was invoked in
vain ; Lord Exmouth was inexorable. The Princess
sent the greater part of her baggage to the Goletta,
the British merchants hastened to embark on board
the vessels of the squadron, the men-of-war were
prepared for action, and the Bey did his best to collect
all available reinforcements. The excitement in
Tunis was immense, and a pacific solution was considered almost impossible. On the 16th Lord
Exmouth, accompanied by Mr. Consul-General
Oglander and his staff, proceeded to the Bardo
Palace. The flagstaff of the British Agency was
previously lowered to indicate a resolution to resort
to an appeal to arms in case of failure, and the
Princess of Wales expected every hour to be arrested
as a hostage. The antecedents of the Bey were not
precisely calculated to assuage her alarm, but Mahmūd
sent one of his officers to assure her that, come what
might, he should never dream of violating the Moslem

laws of hospitality. While the messenger was still
with her, Lord Exmouth entered the room and
announced the satisfactory termination of his mission.
On the following morning the Bey signed a Treaty
whereby in the name of the Regency he abolished
Christian slavery throughout his dominions. Among
the reasons which induced the Bey to yield to the
pressure used by Lord Exmouth was the detention of
the Sultan's envoy, bearing the imperial firman and
robe of investiture, at Syracuse. The Neapolitan
Government would not allow him to depart until the
news of the successful result of the British mission
had arrived, and Mahmūd felt it impossible to forego
the official recognition of his suzerain." [1]

The wife of George IV. was extremely angry at
being interrupted in a delightful course of entertain-
ments, and picnics among the ruins of Carthage and
the orange groves, whither she repaired in the Bey's
coach and six, escorted by sixty memlūks. The
Tunisians were, of course, indignant at the Bey's surrender, nor did piracy cease on account of the Treaty.
Holland, indeed, repudiated the blackmail in 1819,
but Sweden still paid a species of tribute in the form
of one hundred and twenty-five cannons in 1827.

Having gained his point at Tunis and Tripoli
—a most unexpected triumph — Lord Exmouth
came back to Algiers, and endeavoured to negotiate the same concessions there, coolly taking up
his position within short range of the batteries.
His proposals were indignantly rejected, and he
was personally insulted ; two of his officers were

----

[1] BROADLEY, 85-6.

dragged from their horses by the mob, and marched through the streets with their hands tied behind their backs ; the consul, Mr. McDonell, was put under guard, and his wife and other ladies of his family were ignominiously driven into the town from the country house.[1] Lord Exmouth had no instructions for such an emergency ; he arranged that ambassadors should be sent from Algiers to London and Constantinople to discuss his proposal ; and then regretfully sailed for England. He had hardly returned when news arrived of extensive massacres of Italians living under British protection at Bona and Oran by order of the Dey—an order actually issued while the British admiral was at Algiers. Lord Exmouth was immediately instructed to finish his work. On the 25th of July in the same year his flagship, the *Queen Charlotte*, 108, led a squadron of eighteen men of war, of from ten to one hundred and four guns, and including three seventy-fours, out of Portsmouth harbour. At Gibraltar the Dutch admiral, Baron Van Capellan, begged to be allowed to join in the attack with six vessels, chiefly thirty-sixes, and when the time came he fought his ships admirably. On the 27th of August they arrived in the roads of Algiers. The *Prometheus* had been sent ahead to bring off the consul McDonell and his family. Captain Dashwood succeeded in bringing Mrs. and Miss McDonell on board ; but a second boat was less fortunate : the consul's baby took the opportunity of crying just as it was being carried in a basket past the sentinel, by the ship's surgeon, who believed he

[1] PLAYFAIR, 256.

had quieted it. The whole party were taken before the Dey, who, however, released all but the boat's crew, and, as "a solitary instance of his humanity," sent the baby on board. The Consul-General himself remained a prisoner.

No reply being vouchsafed to his flag of truce, Lord Exmouth bore up to the attack, and the *Queen Charlotte* dropped anchor in the entrance of the Mole, some fifty yards off, and was lashed to a mast which was made fast to the shore. A shot from the Mole, instantly answered from the flagship, opened the battle. "Then commenced a fire," wrote the admiral, "as animated and well-supported as I believe was ever witnessed, from a quarter before three till nine, without intermission, and which did not cease altogether till half-past eleven [P M.]. The ships immediately following me were admirably and coolly taking up their stations, with a precision even beyond my most sanguine hope; and never did the British flag receive, on any occasion, more zealous and honourable support.

"The battle was fairly at issue between a handful of Britons, in the noble cause of Christianity, and a horde of fanatics, assembled round their city, and enclosed within its fortifications, to obey the dictates of their Despot. The cause of God and humanity prevailed; and so devoted was every creature in the fleet, that even British women served at the same guns with their husbands, and, during a contest of many hours, never shrank from danger, but animated all around them."

Some of the men-of-war, especially the *Impregnable,*

Rear-Admiral Milne, were hard beset ; but about ten o'clock at night the main batteries were silenced, and in a state of ruin, and "all the ships in the port, with the exception of the outer frigate [which had been boarded], were in flames, which extended rapidly over the whole arsenal, storehouses, and gun-boats, exhibiting a spectacle of awful grandeur and interest no pen can describe." [1] At one o'clock everything in the Marine seemed on fire : two ships wrapped in flames drifted out of the port. Heavy thunder, lightning, and rain, increased the lurid effect of the scene.

Next morning, says Mr. Shaler, "the combined fleets are at anchor in the bay, apparently little damaged ; every part of the town appeared to have suffered. The Marine batteries are in ruins, and may be occupied without any effort. Lord Exmouth holds the fate of Algiers in his hands."

Instead, however, of demolishing the last vestige of the fortifications, and exacting pledges for future good behaviour, the admiral concluded a treaty by which prisoners of war in future should be exchanged and not enslaved ; and the whole of the slaves in Algiers, to the number of 1,642 (chiefly Italian, only

[1] Lord Exmouth's Despatch, August 26, 1816. See also the American Consul Shaler's Report to his Government, September 13th, quoted by Playfair, 269-72. The bombardment destroyed a large part of Mr. Shaler's house, and shells were perpetually whizzing by his ears. His report is full of graphic details, and he was always a true friend of the unlucky McDonell. It is stated that the fleet fired 118 tons of powder, 50,000 shot, nearly 1,000 shells, &c. The English lost 128 killed and 690 wounded. The admiral was wounded in three places, his telescope broken in his hand, and his coat cut to strips. Nor was the Dey less forward at the post of danger.

eighteen English), were at once set at liberty, and the Dey was made to refund the money, amounting to nearly four hundred dollars, which he had that year extorted from the Italian States. Finally, he was made to publicly apologize to the unfortunate McDonell, who had been confined during the siege half naked in the cell for condemned murderers, loaded with chains, fastened to the wall, exposed to the heavy rain, and momentarily expecting his doom. He was now reinstated, and publicly thanked by the admiral.

It was, indeed, satisfactory to have at last administered some salutary discipline to the insolent robbers of Algiers ; but it had been well if the lesson had been final. Their fleet was certainly gone : they had but two vessels left. Their fortifications were severely damaged, but these were soon repaired. No doubt it was no small advantage to have demonstrated that their batteries could be turned and silenced ; but it would have been better to have taken care that they should never mount another gun. Even the moral effect of the victory seems to have been shortlived, for when, in 1819, in pursuance of certain resolutions expressed at the Congress of Aix-la-Chapelle (1818) the French and English admirals delivered " identical notes" to the new Dey, that potentate replied after his manner by throwing up earthworks.

As a matter of fact the same course of insolence and violence continued after the Battle of Algiers as before. Free European girls were carried off by the Dey ; the British consulate was forced open, and even the women's rooms searched ; Mr. McDonell was still victimized ; and the diplomacy and a little fancy firing of Sir Harry Neale in 1824 failed to produce the least effect. Mr. McDonell had to be recalled, and the Dey as usual had his own way. Nothing but downright conquest could stop the plague, and that final measure was reserved for another nation than the English.

XXII.

1830—1881.

THE successes of the English and American fleets had produced their effects, not so much in arresting the course of piracy, as in encouraging the European States to defy the pirates. The *coup de grâce* was administered by France—the *vis-à-vis*, the natural opponent of the Algerine Corsairs, and perhaps the chief sufferer by their attacks. A dispute in April, 1827, between the French consul and the Dey, in which the former forgot the decencies of diplomatic language, and the latter lost his temper and struck the offender with the handle of his fan, led to an ineffectual blockade of Algiers by a French squadron for two years, during which the Algerines aggravated the breach by several acts of barbarity displayed towards French prisoners. Matters grew to a crisis ; in August, 1829, the Dey dismissed a French envoy and fired upon his ship as he was retiring under a flag of truce ; and it became evident that war on a decisive scale was now inevitable.

Accordingly, on May 26th, 1830, a large fleet

sailed out of Toulon. Admiral Duperré commanded, and the land-forces on board numbered thirty-seven thousand foot, besides cavalry and artillery. Delayed by stress of weather, the fleet was not sighted off Algiers till June 13th, when it anchored in the Bay of Sidi Ferrūj, and there landed next day, with little opposition, and began to throw up entrenchments. A force of Arabs and Kabyles was severely defeated on the 19th, with the loss of their camp and provisions, and the French slowly pushed their way towards the city, beating back the Algerines as they advanced. The defenders fought game to the last, but the odds were overwhelming, and the only wonder is that so overpowering a force of besiegers, both by sea and land, should have evinced so much caution and diffidence of their own immense superiority. On July 4th, the actual bombardment of the city began; the Fort de l'Empereur was taken, after the Algerines had blown up the powder magazine; and the Dey asked for terms of surrender. Safety of person and property for himself and for the inhabitants of the city was promised by the French commander, and on this condition the enemy occupied Algiers on the following day, July 5th. A week later the Dey, with his family and attendants and belongings, sailed for Naples in a French frigate, and Algiers had seen the last of its Mohammedan rulers.[1]

Here, so far as Algiers is concerned, the Story of

[1] See the graphic journal of the British Consul-General, R. W. St. John, published in Sir R. LAMBERT PLAYFAIR's *Scourge of Christendom*, pp. 310-322.

the Corsairs properly ends. But a glance at the events which have occurred during the French occupation may usefully supplement what has already been recorded. The conquest had been marked by a moderation and humanity which did infinite honour to the French arms; it would have been well if a similar policy had distinguished their subsequent proceedings. It is not necessary to dwell upon the assurance given by France to Great Britain that the occupation was only temporary ; upon the later announcement of permanent annexation ; or upon England's acquiescence in the perfidy, upon the French engaging never to push their conquests further to the east or west of Algiers—an engagement curiously illustrated by the recent occupation of Tunis. But if the aggrandisement of France in North Africa is matter for regret, infinitely more to be deplored is the manner in which the possession of the interior of the country has been effected. It is not too much to say that from the moment when the French, having merely taken the city of Algiers, began the work of subduing the tribes of the interior in 1830, to the day when they at last set up civil, instead of military, government, after the lessons of the Franco-German war in 1870, the history of Algeria is one long record of stupidly brutal camp-rule, repudiation of sacred engagements, inhuman massacres of unoffending natives of both sexes and all ages, violence without judgment, and severity without reason. One French general after another was sent out to bring the rebellious Arabs and Kabyles into subjection, only to display his own incompetence for the inhuman task,

and to return baffled and brutalized by the disgrace-
ful work he thought himself bound to carry out.
There is no more humiliating record in the annals of
annexation than this miserable conquest of Algiers.
It is the old story of trying to govern what the con-
querors call " niggers," without attempting to understand the people first.   Temper, justice, insight, and
conciliation would have done more in four years than
martial intolerance and drum tyranny accomplished
in forty.

In all these years of miserable guerilla warfare, in
which such well-known commanders as Bugeaud,
Pelissier, Canrobert, St. Arnaud, MacMahon, and
many more, learned their first demoralizing lessons
in warfare, the only people who excite our interest
and admiration are the Arab tribes.   That they were
unwise in resisting the inevitable is indisputable ; but
it is no less certain that they resisted with splendid
valour and indomitable perseverance.   Again and
again they defeated the superior forces of France in
the open field, wrested strong cities from the enemy,
and even threatened to extinguish the authority of
the alien in Algiers for ever.   For all which the
invaders had only to thank themselves.   Had
General Clausel, the first military governor of Algiers,
been a wise man, the people might have accepted,
by degrees, the sovereignty of France.   But the
violence of his measures, and his ignorance of the very
word " conciliation," raised up such strenuous opposition, engendered such terrible reprisals, and set the two
parties so hopelessly against each other, that nothing
less than a prolonged struggle could be expected.

The hero of this sanguinary conflict was 'Abd-el-
Kādir, a man who united in his person and character
all the virtues of the old Arabs with many of the
best results of civilization. Descended from a saintly
family, himself learned and devout, a Hāj or Meccan
pilgrim ; frank, generous, hospitable ; and withal a
splendid horseman, redoubtable in battle, and fired
with the patriotic enthusiasm which belongs to a
born leader of men, 'Abd-el-Kādir became the
recognized chief of the Arab insurgents. The Dey
of Algiers had foreseen danger in the youth, who
was forced to fly to Egypt in fear of his life. When
he returned, a young man of twenty-four, he found
his country in the hands of the French, and his
people driven to desperation. His former fame and
his father's name were talismans to draw the
impetuous tribes towards him; and he soon had
so large a following that the French deemed it
prudent for the moment to recognize him (1834)
as Emīr of Maskara, his native place, of which he
had already been chosen king by general acclamation. Here he prepared for the coming struggle ;
and when the French discovered a pretext for
attacking him in 1835, they were utterly routed on
the river Maska. The fortunes of war vacillated in
the following year, till in May, 1837, 'Abd-el-Kādir
triumphantly defeated a French army in the plain
of the Metija. A fresh expedition of twenty thousand met with no better success, for Arabs and
Berbers are hard to trap, and 'Abd-el-Kādir, whose
strategy evoked the admiration of the Duke of
Wellington, was for a time able to baffle all the

21

marshals of France. The whole country, save a
few fortified posts, was now under his sway, and
the French at last perceived that they had to deal
with a pressing danger. They sent out eighty
thousand men under Marshal Bugeaud, and the
success of this officer's method of sweeping the
country with movable columns was soon apparent.
Town after town fell; tribe after tribe made terms;
even 'Abd-el-Kādir's capital, Takidemt, was destroyed; Maskara was subdued (1841); and the
heroic chief, still repudiating defeat, retreated to
Morocco. Twice he led fresh armies into his own
land, in 1843 and 1844; the one succumbed to the
Duc d'Aumale, the other to Bugeaud. Pelissier
covered himself with peculiar glory by smoking
five hundred men, women, and children to death in
a cave. At last, seeing the hopelessness of further
efforts and the misery they brought upon his people,
'Abd-el-Kādir accepted terms (1847), and surrendered to the Duc d'Aumale on condition of being
allowed to retire to Alexandria or Naples. It is
needless to add that, in accordance with Algerian
precedent, the terms of surrender were subsequently
repudiated, though not by the Royal Duke, and the
noble Arab was consigned for five years to a French
prison. Louis Napoleon eventually allowed him to
depart to Brusa, and he finally died at Damascus
in 1883, not, however, before he had rendered signal
service to his former enemies by protecting the
Christians during the massacres of 1860.

Though 'Abd-el-Kādir had gone, peace did not
settle upon Algeria. Again and again the tribes

revolted, only to feel once more the merciless severity of their military rulers. French colonists did not readily adopt the new field for emigration. It seemed as though the best thing would be to withdraw from a bootless, expensive, and troublesome venture. Louis Napoleon, however, when he visited Algiers in 1865, contrived somewhat to reassure the Kabyles, while he guaranteed their undisturbed possession of their territories; and until his fall there was peace. But the day of weakness for France was the opportunity for Algiers, and another serious revolt broke out; the Kabyles descended from their mountains, and Gen. Durieu had enough to do to hold them in check. The result of this last attempt, and the change of government in France, was the appointment of civil instead of military governors, and since then Algeria has on the whole remained tranquil, though it takes an army of fifty thousand men to keep it so. There are at least no more Algerine Corsairs.

It remains to refer to the affairs of Tunis. If there was provocation for the French occupation of Algiers in 1830, there was none for that of Tunis in 1881.[1] It was a pure piece of aggression, stimulated by the rival efforts of Italy, and encouraged by the timidity of the English Foreign Office, then under the guidance of Lord Granville. A series of diplomatic grievances, based upon no valid grounds, was set up by the ingenious representative of France in the Regency—M. Théodore Roustan,

[1] For a full account of this scandalous proceeding, see Mr. A. M. BROADLEY'S *Tunis, Past and Present.*

since deservedly exposed — and the resistance of
the unfortunate Bey, Mohammed Es-Sādik, to
demands which were in themselves preposterous, and
which obviously menaced his semi-independence as a
viceroy of the Ottoman Empire, received no support
from any of the Powers, save Turkey, who was then
depressed in influence and resources by the adver-
sities of the Russian invasion. The result was
natural : a strong Power, unchecked by efficient
rivals, pursued her stealthy policy of aggression
against a very weak, but not dishonest, State ; and
finally seized upon the ridiculous pretext of some
disturbances among the tribes bordering on Algeria
to invade the territory of the Bey. In vain
Mohammed Es-Sādik assured M. Roustan that
order had been restored among the tribes ; in
vain he appealed to all the Powers, and, above all,
to England. Lord Granville believed the French
Government when it solemnly assured him that " the
operations about to commence on the borderland
between Algeria and Tunis are meant solely to put
an end to the constant inroads of the frontier clans
into Algerian territory, and that the independence of
the Bey and the integrity of his territory are in no
way threatened." It was Algiers over again, but
with even more serious consequences to English
influence—indeed to all but French influence—in the
Mediterranean. " Perfide Albion " wholly confided
in " Perfida Gallia," and it was too late to protest
against the flagrant breach of faith when the French
army had taken Kef and Tabarka (April 26, 1881),
when the tricolor was floating over Bizerta, and

when General Bréart, with every circumstance of insolent brutality, had forced the Treaty of Kasr-es-Sa'íd upon the luckless Bey under the muzzles of the guns of the Republic (May 12th). It is difficult to believe that the feeling of the English statesmen of the day is expressed in the words—*Haec olim meminisse juvabit.*

The Bey had been captured—he and since his death Sidi.'Alí Bey have continued to be the figure-heads of the French Protectorate--but his people were not so easily subdued. The southern provinces of Tunis broke into open revolt, and for a time there ensued a period of hopeless anarchy, which the French authorities made no effort to control. At last they bestirred themselves, and to some purpose. Sfax was mercilessly bombarded and *sacked,* houses were blown up with their inhabitants inside them, and a positive reign of terror was inaugurated, in which mutual reprisals, massacres, and executions heightened the horrors of war. The whole country outside the fortified posts became the theatre of bloodshed, robbery, and anarchy. It was the history of Algiers *in petto.* Things have slowly improved since then, especially since M. Roustan's recall ; doubtless in time Tunis will be as subdued and as docile as Algiers ; and meanwhile France is developing the resources of the land, and opening out one of the finest harbours in existence. Yet M. Henri de Rochefort did not, perhaps, exaggerate when he wrote : "We compared the Tunisian expedition to an ordinary fraud. We were mistaken. The Tunis business is a robbery aggravated by murder." The

"Algerian business" was of a similar character. *Qui commence bien finit bien,* assumes Admiral Jurien de la Gravière in his chapter entitled "Gallia Victrix." If the history of France in Africa ends in bringing the southern borderlands of the Mediterranean, the old haunts of the Barbary Corsairs, within the pale of civilization, it may some day be possible to bury the unhappy past, and inscribe upon the tombstone the optimistic motto : *Finis coronat opus.*

THE END.

INDEX.